# OKLAHOMA

## RODEO WOMEN

TRACEY HANSHEW

THE
History
PRESS

Published by The History Press
Charleston, SC
www.historypress.com

First published 2020

Manufactured in the United States

ISBN 9781467139151

Library of Congress Control Number: 2019951839

*Notice*: The information in this book is true and complete to the best of our knowledge. It is offered without guarantee on the part of the author or The History Press. The author and The History Press disclaim all liability in connection with the use of this book.

*This book is dedicated to all women in Oklahoma, past and present, who support the rodeo industry and preserve the rich heritage of ranching and rodeo in Oklahoma.*

# CONTENTS

# ACKNOWLEDGEMENTS

This book would not have been possible without the support of many people. I especially appreciate the generous donation of photos from the Gilcrease Museum and the expediency with which Diana M. Cox, intellectual property and copyright manager, processed my request. For donating photos from the National Cowboy & Western Heritage Museum and the support there for both photo requests and assistance with research materials, thank you to Kera Newby, digital and manuscript archivist for the Donald C. and Elizabeth M. Dickinson Research Center.

The wonderful photos and research information from the Oklahoma History Society (Carolyn Krumanocker and Rachel Mosman, researchers) and the Museum of the Great Plains (Deborah Anna Baroff, senior curator) allowed for the personalized stories that make this book true to the nature of rodeo, which is really a history of people who helped make Oklahoma the center of equine interest. Many of the women in this book are already recognized for their lifetime achievements in rodeo, ranching and equine industries as honorees of the National Cowgirl Museum and Hall of Fame. I am grateful for the support and advice from Bethany Dodson, research and education manager at the National Cowgirl Museum and Hall of Fame. Her assiduousness ensures records of women important to the American West are accessible for study. I appreciate the research support and efforts of all these organizations and the women listed here who help ensure that the women important to the history of rodeo and the far-reaching West will not be forgotten.

# INTRODUCTION

**W**omen have long been a significant part of development and progress in American history. In a place like Oklahoma that has a richly diverse past, it has perhaps required a bit more from its women than other states, as the transition from territory to state in Oklahoma was as politically rocky as it was literally a harsh climate to endure. Oklahoma has some of the most extreme weather in the United States, and for ranching folk it requires perseverance. But ranchers in Oklahoma not only endured, they flourished. When rodeo formed, Oklahomans provided a significant portion of contestants, livestock, judges, organizers and workers to both promote and sustain the sport. As in much of American history, women have played a part all along. This book tells the story of how women in Oklahoma were historically important to rodeo. Although some of the women featured here were not born in Oklahoma, they contributed to rodeo in Oklahoma or national rodeo through their actions in Oklahoma or in relation to Oklahoma.[1] As competitors, women have historically had an erratic relationship with rodeo, but like many early histories that overlooked women's contributions to America, women advanced rodeo in more ways than as athletes. Many women participated in rodeo "firsts" both in and outside the arena through supporting roles as mothers. Their duties are not that different from moms of competitors in other sports or 4-H (youth clubs for agricultural communities). Most are early risers ensuring both kids and animals are fed, driving all over creation to make playdays (practice rodeo-type events for kids) and Little Britches rodeos (loading, unloading, saddling and unsaddling before kids are big enough) and double-checking cinches and tack when their kids are old enough to do it themselves. Women also help run the ranches that produce the livestock for rodeo and raise the cowboys and cowgirls who compete. Women marry into rodeo, becoming the wives who wait by the phone praying for a good call or the bleacher wives who cheer or record videos at countless rodeos along the road. Women oftentimes are bookkeepers and secretaries, deliver first aid, write checks and now are also arena pickup men (this term does not seem to have been updated even though women have performed this job since at least the 1910s, but it needs to be; perhaps rodeo should use the term "pickup rider") and are award-winning stock contractors. So, women have promoted rodeo as superstars during the golden age of rodeo and supported it in many ways behind the scenes as well. This book explores how women in Oklahoma have been an integral part of professional equine sports and have contributed to the rodeo industry from its inception. Oklahoma's central location, strong heritage in ranching and rodeo history situate this state in a unique position to the overall sport and business. For this reason, as well as to review the incredible accomplishments of these women in rodeo, a study of their achievements is overdue. From cowgirls like Lucille Mulhall, who helped women move from ranching into professional competition, or Mildred Chrisman, who helped promote women in rodeo during the Depression, to the groundbreaking accomplishments of modern cowgirl Maggie Parker, who was the first to earn prize money for winning a Professional Rodeo Cowboys Association (PRCA) bucking event, these women have proven important to rodeo and the related professions that support it.

Chapter 1 covers the history of rodeo and discusses the diverse types of rodeo and organizations that support it. It also includes how Oklahoma has supported rodeo through equine trades. Chapter 2 gives an account of Oklahoma's most famous cowgirl, Lucille Mulhall. Chapter 3 moves into discussion about those record breakers or firsts from rodeo women. During the Great Depression and World War II, rodeo, like much of the country, faced challenging times. Chapter 4 looks at how Oklahoma cowgirls and women working through the community kept rodeo going and combined that goal with their activities to support the war effort. Women were then pushed to the fringes of rodeo events and relegated to the single event of barrel racing. But consistent with the cowgirl grit that inspired women to work in early ranching and later find their way into rodeo competition, that same determination led women to form their own professional organization to be able to continue rodeo careers in the events of their choosing. Finally, chapter 6 looks at women's involvement in rodeo and related businesses today and offers some concluding thoughts.

There are countless Oklahoman women who have participated and continue to work to promote rodeo and the rodeo family's way of life, and although not all made it into this book, it is respectfully dedicated to them. They made this history with their efforts behind the chutes, in the stands and in full center arena to shape this important heritage and continuing legacy of Oklahoma.

Chapter 1

# RODEO ROOTS

R odeo began on ranches across the American West and became popular when rural people gathered to watch competitions between ranch outfits or people working for the ranch, often cowboys or vaqueros who worked cattle. Audience curiosity and admiration for the cowboys and cowgirls who competed in spectacular events transformed rodeo until over time, it grew in popularity. Both the number and size of rodeos increased, expanding into the business it is today, which spans the United States, Canada and internationally. Steeped in interest in both the competition and nostalgia for the Old West, rodeo is a sport intertwined with hardworking people and the animals that sustained America's westward expansion. Wild West shows and rodeo retell the stories of the West through a unique form of entertainment, providing exciting real-life examples of a life long ago. Because this sport originated with ranching, most athletes also come from a ranch background; there have, however, been stars from areas outside the rural West. Tillie Baldwin immigrated to the United States from Arendal, Norway, and was a Lady Bronc Riding Champ as well as an All-Around World Champion in 1912 and 1913. Six-time National Finals Rodeo (NFR) qualifier Bobby Delvecchio, from the Bronx, New York, and Los Angeles–born Charlie Sampson, the first African American world champion bull rider (1982), are among those who proved that one does not have to be born into rodeo to become a successful athlete in the sport.[2]

On ranches across the West, where cowhand competitions began and the reward for winning consisted of bragging rights about being a top roper or bronc rider, competitions during the late 1800s were known by various names, including bronc shows, cowboy tournaments, roundup (separate from the actual rounding up or gathering of herds of cattle on ranches but often occurring during or near the time to collect cattle from distant pastures) and Texas picnics.[3] The word *rodeo* is Spanish and was used by vaqueros well before Anglo encroachment into the West. One explanation about how the name *rodeo* became synonymous with today's competition derives from California about thirty years after the first organized contest. Willard H. Porter, in "The American Rodeo, Sport and Spectacle," offers that the word *rodeo* became the one that stuck after a 1912 roundup show held in Los Angeles that included "mostly Mexican kids" who could not say the word "roundup" and replaced it with "rodeo," which is the Spanish word for roundup.[4] From that point, the use of most other terms faded. Although rodeo did not begin in Oklahoma, when it caught on, Oklahoma was all in. Today across the state, a variety of rodeos occurs weekly, making Oklahoma a significant contributor to the rodeo industry.

Contests at ranch rodeos most closely resemble early ranching and spring roundup contests. Ranch rodeos require contestants to be employed on a ranch and the ranch hands enter as a team or outfit representing the ranch they work for. These events stay truer to real ranch work and include "calf branding" (using chalk or chalk paint), steer "mugging" (throwing and tying a yearling steer), wild cow milking, team roping and team penning.[5] Some ranch rodeos include variations like bucking events. A few professional rodeos, like the 101 Rodeo in Ponca City, pay tribute to ranching and local ranch workers by beginning the rodeo with a separate ranch rodeo buck out exhibition before the professional competition begins. Ranch rodeo roughstock events have slightly different rules and use altered rigging for saddle broncs, and some use the same equipment for work on the ranch.[6] Ranch rodeos have produced professional rodeo contestants, but many contestants keep their full-time ranch jobs and attend rodeos closer to home, like the Green County Classic Ranch Rodeo in Claremore or the Waurika Chamber of Commerce Ranch Rodeo in Waurika. Scheduling for ranch rodeos is regional, limiting the tour radius to an area more realistic for full-time cowhands to compete without having to leave ranching and family to travel the great distances required for the professional circuit. Much like the organizations that support other rodeos, ranch rodeo has locally based supporters, including the "Oklahoma Cattlemen's Association, the American Cowboy Ranch Rodeo Association, the Working Cowboys Rodeo Association, and the

Cowgirls at the 101 Ranch. *101 Ranch Collection. Cowgirls Mirror Image at 101, GM 4327.8317. Gilcrease Museum Archives.*

Oklahoma Ranch Rodeo Cowboys Association."[7] These organizations help promote the lifestyle and the rodeo community, and most lead up to a final rodeo at the end of the season to name the top athletes in each event for the year.

In the approximately 135 years of rodeo history, it has only been professionalized for about 85 years.[8] The Professional Rodeo Cowboys Association (PRCA) annually awards the best rodeos in the United States by venue or size category: Largest Outdoor Rodeo, Small Rodeo of the Year, Medium Rodeo of the Year and Largest Indoor Rodeo of the Year. Professionalization helped to standardize rodeo by hosting contests that consistently included the same events: bareback bronc riding, saddle bronc riding, calf roping, steer roping, team roping, trick riding, fancy roping, bulldogging (also known as steer wrestling), barrel racing and bull riding. Smaller rodeos in rural communities consistently prove important in rodeo not only as part of the history but also as an opportunity for local ranchers to get into rodeo and sustain the ties with communities. Additionally, these rodeos are often as exciting and sometimes showcase equally competitive animals and athletes as any large rodeo. This is evident in the recognition of local rodeos like the winner of the 2018 Small Rodeo of the Year, the Will Rogers Stampede in Claremore, Oklahoma. For most of the sport's history, the greatest percentage of rodeos have not been the large shows with big money, blitz and bling that many of the PRCA and National Finals rodeos are today but local rodeo closer to its ranching roots.

As rodeo expanded and became more organized, a tour or route formed that contestants followed on their travels to the top rodeos. Clifford P. Westermeier describes a grand circuit as consisting of a season running from January until mid-December and covering three geographical phases. Phase one would be the Northwest, phase two through the Midwest and phase three in southern areas. Within these geographic regions, contestants traveled to compete in at least three large shows within a five-hundred-mile area and often participated in many small rodeos along the road as time would allow. The Midwest region included Oklahoma, where contestants competed in now well-known rodeos like Ada, the Elks Rodeo in Woodward and the Will Rogers Memorial Rodeo in Vinita.[9] Today, as part of the National Circuit System, this regional tour is called the Prairie Circuit and encompasses Kansas, Oklahoma and Nebraska. Each regional circuit hosts PRCA-sanctioned rodeos, and points count toward PRCA year-end totals as well as those tallied within each circuit. Divisions like the Prairie Circuit also host annual finals. The Prairie Circuit finals are in October each year, with the finals headquartered in Duncan, Oklahoma.[10]

The first rodeo in Oklahoma began sometime in the mid-1880s, and as with most rodeo histories, it was a competition between ranch outfits. In sparsely populated areas like the Panhandle and western Oklahoma, rodeo provided an occasion to gather and socialize. In Benton, the legend goes that one year in the 1880s, after the yearly roundup, cowboys at the saloon were talking about Buffalo Bill's Wild West Show, run by Bill Cody and started in 1883. When one cowboy who had ridden in Cody's show said local cowboys in Benton were "just as good [as the] cowboys…in the show," the idea came to light to create a local Wild West show. According to Donald E. Green, "The primary objective…[was] to put on a show for the grangers and especially for their pretty daughters, for the range men wanted to get better acquainted with them."[11] Benton then was likely the first rodeo in the Oklahoma Panhandle, and events consisted of contests in bronc riding and steer roping. There were two teams with six men per team for the bronc-riding event. Like in today's wild horse races, animals were not held in a chute for the rider to mount. This event required teams to select and rope a horse from a herd of untamed stock and then to saddle, bridle and ride the wild horse. One team member would "ear down" the horse while the others helped saddle it. Then one cowboy would mount and ride the bronc to a "finish line about 100 yards away." On the occasion of the first such event, a cowboy named "Irish McGovern won first place riding a mustang named Soda Biscuit."[12] A similar competition held at Hardesty in 1891 interested neighboring Texas cowboys from the "Diamond Tail outfit in the southeastern Texas Panhandle, [who] rode up to the Strip to compete with the local boys."[13] The idea caught on, and rodeo spread first through Beaver County and then the rest of the Oklahoma Panhandle and beyond. By 1891, areas like Vinita, El Reno and Shawnee had begun hosting annual competitions after each spring roundup.

In 1903, rodeo producers eager to attract large crowds selected dates for these contests to coincide with other major events like the Oklahoma Cattlemen's Convention. The result: twenty thousand people attended the contest in Oklahoma City.[14] When the 101 Ranch hosted a spectacular event in June 1905 for the convention of the National Editorial Association, which convened in Guthrie, Oklahoma Territory, more than eleven thousand people attended.[15] The McDermott Grove Fourth of July celebrations had been an annual event since the 1890s, and in 1908, for the festivities, citizens of Texas County also planned to commemorate earlier ranchers in the territory. The Cow-Boy Reunion and Frontier Days Celebration took place in Guymon from March 31 through April 2, 1910. The rodeo featured a "cow pony race…barrel race, cigar race, potatoe [*sic*] race, hat race, ladies horse race, roping contest, riding contest, wild horse race, steer riding… and a fancy and trick roping exhibition."[16] Like many early rodeos, smaller rodeos in rural areas did not occur in the dirt arenas used today but rather in open pasture areas encircled by spectators, wagons and cars. Until 1919, no rodeos, large or small, used stock chutes. The Panhandle rodeos and Fourth of July celebrations as annual events melded rodeo and patriotism with ranch life, establishing a sentiment about rodeo that remains largely unchanged over the years.

Rancher Charlie Hitch, well known throughout the Oklahoma Panhandle, held Fourth of July barbecues that included a chuck wagon and campfire-cooked meals, plus rodeos on his ranch. They were an annual highlight of Texas County. Charlie, who hosted nostalgic "old-fashioned" roundups near his ranch, held them in Cedar Canyon, where most of the participants were "the old-timers who still had the strength to rope a steer, stretch him out, and brand him."[17] The legacy of Charlie Hitch's roundups combined with the McDermott Grove celebrations culminated in the Pioneer Days celebration at Guymon in 1933. The date chosen for the Guymon Pioneer Days was May 2 to commemorate the passage of the "Organic Act of May 2, 1890, which had authorized the establishment of the Oklahoma Territory and attached

Cowgirls from the 101 Ranch, *left to right*: the Parry sisters, Martha Schultz and Bessie Herberg, 1916. *101 Ranch Collection. GM 4327.9036. Gilcrease Museum Archives.*

the Panhandle to that territorial government."[18] Honoring this heritage, and recognizing the importance of ranchers to the community, the 1940 Pioneer Days celebration provided free admission to "pioneers who had lived in the county for at least fifty years."[19] Although interest in cowgirls and cowboys grew from the late 1800s to the 1910s, they participated/contested only part time because rodeos were not held often enough to make a full-time career. That changed by the 1920s during the golden age of sport, which included a golden age of rodeo, during which time cowboys and cowgirls became nationally recognized stars. Over time, rodeos in Oklahoma became more numerous.

The frequency of rodeo activities in Oklahoma, including roping, barrel racing and playdays, created opportunities to help support early rodeo careers because events occurred in "every town of any size…and these organizations provided grassroots support for amateur rodeos and developed a host of riding and roping contests from which sprang numerous Oklahoma rodeo champions," creating a supply and support system for rodeo consisting of more than one "hundred of these organizations" that continues today.[20] Oklahoma developed many well-known rodeos like the Dewey Roundup (1908–50s), the Tulsa Stampede (1934–84) and the now famous Cavalcade, held in Pawhuska every year since 1947. Cavalcade has hosted as many as "seventy-five roundup clubs and thousands of spectators," making it the largest amateur rodeo in Oklahoma and one often advertised as the largest in the world.[21]

As rodeo grew, training schools began expanding opportunities to potential athletes outside of rural ranching by opening the schools to anyone interested. Teaching those who had not grown up in ranching to become rodeo contestants and helping those who wanted to improve their athletic skills, these training schools impacted growth in the rodeo community. There were also unofficial schools in places like Ponca City at the 101 Ranch, where future Wild West show performers would work on the ranch as a segue into shows, rodeo competition or, later, motion pictures. Rich easterners who could afford a working vacation also stayed at the 101 and learned ranch work "just for the fun of it."[22] The idea of rodeo schools spread to other states, but by the 1940s, Oklahoma schools consistently produced champions as more formal training centers opened. For example, six-time world steer roping champion Everett Shaw and four-time world champion steer roper Shoat Webster honed their skills roping at Fred Lowry's Ranch School near Lenapah, Oklahoma.[23] Some contestants opened their own schools, like five-time all-around world champion Jim Shoulders, who, in 1962, began

Teenager Wyatt Christian from Morrison, Oklahoma, driving a team in the Cavalcade Parade at Pawhuska, Oklahoma, July 23, 2016. Wyatt and his family won that year for traveling the greatest distance with horses only, camping two nights on the side of the road to get to the rodeo from Morrison. *Photo by author.*

offering "six-day courses in the three riding events at his ranch in Henryetta, Oklahoma," providing training and inspiration to future generations who admired the accomplished cowboy.[24] Towns sometimes adopted favorite rodeo stars and put up signs or billboards to declare themselves as the home of famous cowboys and cowgirls, and one even changed its name. In 1942, Berwyn, Oklahoma, became Gene Autry, Oklahoma.[25]

Rodeo's success today is still reliant on ranching culture and production. To consider Oklahoma's role in supporting rodeo requires a look at the entire equine industry: farming, ranching, breeding, training, veterinary services, equipment, tack and supply, transportation and facilities. Modern ranchers may get by with four-wheelers or ATVs to move cattle, but rodeo cannot exist without horses, and Oklahoma plays a vital role in that supply. For comparison, Texas is over 268,581 square miles and Oklahoma 68,667 square miles, and while Texas and many other western states also are heavily invested in equine industry, Oklahoma ranks second only to Texas in raising American quarter horses, the most popular breed in rodeo's timed events.[26] According to the American Horse Council (AHC), there is an estimated average of twelve horses per household in Oklahoma.[27] Through tourism, business and private ownership, the Oklahoma horse industry "provides 39,000 jobs working both directly and indirectly with horses [and]… approximately 70 percent of recreational horse owners are involved with some sort of show or competition," which also contributes to the economy.[28] Oklahoma is home to six national equine-related organizations, including the "National Reining Horse Association, Pinto Horse Association, Palomino Horse Breeders of America and Barrel Futurities of America, which employs 119 people."[29] Oklahoma also has nationally recognized training centers that in 2012 hosted 612 national and international equine events. The

Working cowgirls at the 101 Ranch. *101 Ranch Collection. GM 4327.9046. Gilcrease Museum Archives.*

economic impact of just 15 of the national and world-level horse shows held in Oklahoma City is estimated to be "more than $100 million annually," and overall, equine events have "a 1.2-billion-dollar direct impact on the state economy."[30] But the show or rodeo is just one aspect or the fun part of these events and reflects a small fraction of what is necessary to maintain horses. When other factors are included, like "trailer manufacturing businesses, tack and clothing manufacturing businesses and agricultural enterprises" (i.e. feed) and all other activities directly related to horse production and ownership, the contribution to the Oklahoma economy "expands to 3.1 billion dollars."[31] This economic investment combined with generations of family businesses and interest in equine activities in turn leads to an interest in improving said businesses; this is done primarily through educational programs, starting with children in 4-H and similar organizations and going all the way to scholarly research at institutions of higher education.

Oklahoma State University, with its extensive veterinary program, is among "six colleges and universities offering equine-related degree programs" in the state. Higher education programs contribute to state-of-the-art veterinary practices, innovative technology and equine research, and in turn, equine businesses thrive. Improving conditions and quality of horses are "26 equine-assisted therapy operations and 17 equine rescue facilities" in

Oklahoma that also add $5.1 million to the state revenue. The combination of educational interest in equine industries, advanced equine technology, jobs and ranching impacts Oklahoma's participation in and impact on rodeo.[32] The cohesion of these efforts is found in people—those who generate the interest and are committed to work in these fields. Many of them have a direct connection to and therefore a deeper understanding of agriculture and ranching, which also helps them to anticipate the needs of rodeo.

The majority of rodeo athletes have come from ranching backgrounds.[33] While a rodeo event like bull riding does not require a background or even knowledge of ranching skills, the fact remains that many kids from rodeo families or who are inspired by attending rodeo often get their start riding and roping calves when working or playing on family ranches before competing in Little Britches or playday competitions.[34] From kids' competition to amateur contestants, living and working on ranches allows them to practice roping and taking care of cattle, keeping their skills sharp for competition. Consequently, rural areas and those that are largely agriculturally based, like Oklahoma, influence the continuation of new contestants in the sport. This was one factor in the decision to move the PRCA's National Finals Rodeo to Oklahoma City in 1965. Oklahoma could almost guarantee a fan base, particularly given the interest in preserving western heritage. In December 1965, the National Cowboy & Western Heritage Museum was dedicated and opened.[35] Furthermore, both the National Cowboy & Western Heritage Museum and the Oklahoma City Chamber of Commerce sponsored the rodeo. This was by far the most successful of all National Finals Rodeo contests up to that time. The plan to secure Oklahoma City as the permanent site for the annual finale of the professional rodeo season lasted for twenty years, and those years proved critical to the success of the NFR.

The National Finals Rodeo is a season-end contest where the top fifteen contestants in each event compete to determine the world champion for that year. Contestants earn their spots as the top fifteen money winners in the PRCA based on prizes won while competing at sanctioned rodeos across the United States and western Canada, where they earn points to become eligible for the NFR. The NFR began in 1959 in Dallas, Texas, where it stayed for three years, drawing crowds of 54,000 the first year at the Dallas State Fair Grounds but declining to 44,354 the final year in Dallas in 1961.[36] The Finals in Dallas held roughstock events but limited timed events to just two: steer wrestling and calf roping. The Finals for the other timed events— team roping, steer roping and barrel races—were hosted in Clayton, New Mexico, in 1959, and steer roping again was in Clayton in 1960, but the team roping and barrel racing were even farther away from Dallas in Scottsdale, Arizona. In 1961, another move extended the distance from the main event in Dallas when the steer roping finals took place in Laramie, Wyoming, and team roping and barrel racing finals were held in Santa Maria, California.[37] Then, in 1962, the National Finals Rodeo moved to Los Angeles, California. Again, not all events were centrally located, with steer roping in Douglas, Wyoming, and barrel racing back in Dallas, but in Los Angeles, attendance for the first year greatly exceeded what it had been in Texas, with the crowd having multiplied to 68,994.[38] The Finals faced inconsistent financial earnings due to dramatically decreased attendance that over the next two years led to uncertainty about the future of any finals event. In 1963, steer roping finals moved to Pawhuska, Oklahoma, and barrel racing finals once again remained in Dallas, keeping these events more central in geographic location for contestants and fans.

A key development in professional rodeo occurred in 1965, when the NFR moved to the brand-new Jim Norick Arena in Oklahoma City. Steer roping moved again but stayed in Oklahoma, going to Vinita, and barrel racing stayed in Dallas. During its time in Oklahoma, the NFR made changes to help stabilize and grow the Finals rodeo into the spectacular event it is today. The year 1966 brought economic and social change to the PRCA and the Finals. The Finals began to prosper financially, as prize money increased to $54,000, and socially by breaking color barriers when Myrtis Dightman made history as the first African American cowboy to place first in a Finals round of competition. When discussing his journey to the Finals that year, Dightman described how throughout the year, he often rode after the rodeo during re-rides.[39] He stated, "I went to a rodeo in Crockett, Texas, and had a bull that hadn't been ridden. They wouldn't let me ride in the performance, they held me until after the performance. I rode the bull and won the bull riding."[40] Another time in Little Rock, Arkansas, he said, "they wouldn't even let me in the gate. One of the Combs brothers from Oklahoma—I believe it was Tommy—saw me standing there and said, 'Myrtis, the bull riding's going on; what are you doing out here?' I told him, and Tommy told the gate man that I was a contestant and that he'd better let me in. They'd already turned my bull out, but they ran him back in for me and I ended up winning second."[41] As the only "black cowboy at the finals," Dightman placed eighth in the world standings in 1966, winning $9,152. His success was a pivotal moment for black cowboys in professional rodeo.[42]

In 1967, Clem McSpadden, well-known rodeo announcer from Chelsea, Oklahoma, became the new general manager of the NFR. McSpadden changed the advertising methods by promoting the Finals on the radio and having admired world champion Freckles Brown and famous radio commentator Paul Harvey speak about the rodeo. The radio promotions amplified awareness and boosted popularity of the Finals, starting a trend of increasing interest in the NFR that has not subsided. Additionally, McSpadden moved all events except the steer roping (held in McAlester, Oklahoma) to the Oklahoma City location.[43] McSpadden attributed the new success to the Oklahoma location, saying, "Country Western people say the Ryman Auditorium is 'The Mother Church of Country Music.' This building [Jim Norick Arena in Oklahoma City] is the mother church of the National Finals Rodeo. It's where it came of age. It's where all performances became sellouts."[44] The results were unprecedented growth.

Just five years after moving to Oklahoma City, professional rodeo began to expand at a remarkable rate, resulting in increased prize monies for most events. Team roping was an exception; it did relocate to Oklahoma City, but that event did not immediately see adjusted earnings.

In 1972, the Finals rodeo increased the number of contests to ten rounds and increased award earnings for the role of team ropers. Prior to the 1972 National Finals, go-rounds for team ropers paid "just over $300," and when the average pay was only $711, many teams questioned if the NFR was worth the trip to Oklahoma. By 1972, winnings had increased to "over $21,000," greatly improving earnings.[45] At that time, only about one-sixth of the PRCA rodeos offered team roping, but again this change in increasing the Finals prize money made it a pivotal moment for the now wildly popular event. It has expanded to include a Team Roping World Series, an additional and separate competition that coincides with the NFR.[46]

NFR rule changes made during the Oklahoma stint improved the overall quality of the Finals rodeo for both contestants and fans. The previous rule, which awarded the winner determined by total annual earnings alone, left some contestants who qualified for the Finals then, and under that rule, unable to surpass the top contestant, whose earnings may have greatly exceeded a contestant in the fourteenth or fifteenth qualifying position. Any amount won, even if placing first at the National Finals Rodeo, might not have been enough to close the gap and win the title of world champion. The idea was to change the rule so that contestants would all start the final rounds on an equal footing rather than having to play catch-up or working for a "second because the regular-season leader already had the gold buckle bagged."[47] This change intensified competition by challenging "skill under pressure."[48] While this helped level the playing field, it also created a new problem: a potential tie. This phenomenon occurred in the bull riding event in 1977, resulting in a history-making ride-off between bull riders Don Gay and Randy Magers. The two riders tied for the world title after ten rounds, prompting the judges to declare a sudden-death ride-off to determine the world champion, a unique decision. Magers rode first and was bucked off, leaving Gay to ride not for style but just to make the whistle. Gay recalled the negative aspects of the sudden-death rule, stating, "The bad thing about sudden death is that it brings luck into the picture. The world champion should be the cowboy who has the best year. But being in the record books as having taken part in the only ride-off may be the only record that I have that will never be broken."[49] Today, this rule has again been changed, and world champions are determined by "total season earnings at PRCA rodeos across the continent, including monies earned at the Wrangler NFR," which eliminates the possibility of ties.[50]

The success of the National Finals Rodeo during its Oklahoma term also brought other national rodeo championship competitions to the state. In 1984, the PRCA National Finals Steer Roping moved from Laramie, Wyoming, to the Lazy E Arena in Guthrie, Oklahoma. The Women's National Finals Rodeo (WNFR) moved in 1985 from Texas to Oklahoma—also hosted by the Lazy E—where the WNFR stayed until 1993. Oklahoma also hosts the International Finals Rodeo (IFR), "held annually since 1969 by the International Professional Rodeo Association (IPRA), which is based in Oklahoma City."[51] The National Circuit Finals Rodeo first began in 1987 and for the first twenty-four years was hosted by Idaho State University in Pocatello, Idaho. In 2011, it, too, moved to centrally located Oklahoma, hosted in both Oklahoma City and Guthrie until 2015.[52]

Oklahomans committed to rodeo worked together to pitch in and support the business. W.K. Stratton, who grew up around rodeo, recalled that when he was a kid, his mother rodeoed and attended a rodeo every weekend, "maybe one of the Guthrie Roundup Club's rodeos. Or maybe the indoor collegiate rodeos at Oklahoma A&M [now Oklahoma State University] in Stillwater. Or maybe the jackpot rodeos at the Thedford Ranch near the tiny community of Orlando...or maybe the biggest rodeo in the county, the Eighty-Niners' Day Rodeo at Jelsma Stadium in Guthrie."[53] This instilled in Stratton the importance of Oklahoma hosting the NFR. Roundup clubs like the Guthrie Roundup Club helped to sell NFR tickets. Stratton states that "ensuring the NFR's success in Oklahoma had become a matter of state pride." Buying a ticket meant that you "were doing something good for Oklahoma."[54] This proved true, as large gains in rodeo sponsorship increased along with rodeo activity in Oklahoma. With multiple Finals events increasing national awareness and as the NFR's popularity increased, so, too, did commercial sponsorship. In 1982, numerous corporations from all over the United States contributed as much as $2 million to professional rodeo for prize money. Oklahoma even serves as a resting place for rodeo animal greats, providing tombstones for them at the National Cowboy & Western Heritage Museum. Bucking bronc Hell's Angel, rope horse Poker Chip and the great bucking bull Tornado—which bucked off more than two hundred riders and was thought to be un-ridable before Freckles Brown rode him in 1967 at the NFR in Oklahoma City—are memorialized at the museum.[55]

Oklahoma proved to be a prime location to nurture the NFR at a time when the NFR needed it most. Its central location in the United States made it the perfect place to host a true national finals. With also being in the middle of ranch territory and in proximity to the American Quarter Horse Association (AQHA) down the road in Amarillo, Texas, it is understandable that the Finals grew during the Oklahoma years. It is unfortunate that in trying to compete with other venues like Las Vegas, Nevada, the decision to relocate the NFR came down to money. Oklahoma City lost the 1984 bid to keep the NFR over the issue of prize monies and facilities, even with consideration of building a new "thirty-million-dollar arena."[56] The decision to leave Oklahoma, however, was not unanimous. "The rodeo purse at the 1984 NFR in Oklahoma was $900,000, [and] about $200,000 in prize money was awarded to stock contractors."[57] Herb McDonald, then head of Las Vegas Events, made a proposal that included a "guaranteed prize fund of $1.8 million to the cowboys and $700,000 to the contractors," and he included a promise to increase those funds each year. Even with this offer, when the PRCA board voted on the move, it was a tie, 6–6. This left the tiebreaking vote to Shawn Davis, PRCA president; he voted for Las Vegas.[58] Moving because it would "improve the business" of rodeo did not immediately result in the sell-out crowds in Vegas today, but often money is a decider, and the heartland history that founded rodeo has taken a back seat, replaced by city lights and the lure of Vegas.[59] The rodeo road from the pastures of Oklahoma to the pavement of Las Vegas was possible due to the longtime effort of people trying to preserve the NFR along with their western heritage and, for many families, a way of life. None of it would have been possible were it not for the working women who were part of it.

Like the countless often unrecognized women who have been an influence in American history, women who helped build the West have received limited

"Sarah Crutcher, 12-year-old girl herding cattle. Route 4, c/o S.O. Crutcher. She was out of school (#49 Comanche County) only 2 weeks this year and that was to herd 100 head of cattle for her father, a prosperous farmer. She said: 'I didn't like it either.' She is doing well in school. Is in Grade 8." Lewis Wickes Hine, April 1917. 1 photographic print. *Library of Congress Prints and Photographs, Division Washington, D.C. 20540 USA, hdl.loc.gov/loc.pnp/pp.print. LOT 7475, v. 3, no. 4811 [P&P].*

acknowledgement for their contributions in rural development. Providing more than just domestic support, ranch women have worked side by side with men all along. Many learned to rope and ride at an early age, continuing to work outside and as cowhands after marrying and starting families. Even when questions about a woman's proper place came up nationally, rural ranching women made their place outside conventional gender standards. In one example in the Oklahoma Panhandle on the Hitch ranch, daughter Joyce helped with cattle and other ranch duties until she married. After marrying, the family expected that she would stop that type of work. But as her family still needed to drive one hundred head of cattle on horseback from one corner of the ranch to "Uncle Charlie Hitch's wheat pasture, a distance of about ten miles," Joyce planned to help. A family member wrote in her journal that "Joyce would probably not go with the men because she 'would get tired and dusty.' In the margin she later added: 'Joyce went.'"[60] Joyce is an example of many ranch women who worked various jobs outside what was expected of women according to broader social standards. They established a precedent for generations of rural women who developed the idea of cowgirl grit, a character trait often appropriated for and by women who rise above expected limitations to just do what is needed regardless of their sex. This can-do, will-do attitude set rural ranching women apart. They contributed to their rural communities, which included support of the rodeo industry. For ranch women, this was another way of supporting their own family and was therefore, to them, something perfectly natural.

Many ranching women rearing their families while working on a ranch could lull a baby to sleep in the saddle while checking the fences. Many became very skilled ropers and bronc riders and did the same work as the men in their own right. The most well known of these Oklahoma ranch women, Lucille Mulhall, became a key factor in connecting ranch life to professional rodeo competition for women. Furthermore, she added many improvements to rodeo.

Chapter 2

# LUCILLE

It is a bold statement to say that one woman changed the course of rodeo history in Oklahoma, but if anyone fits that description, it is Lucille Mulhall. Lucille is most well known as "America's First Cowgirl," and she gained national attention for her roping skills, which sparked a global interest in the American cowgirl. While Wild West shows had introduced the American public to western women, including some making their names with Oklahoma Wild West shows like the Pawnee Bill Wild West Show and the 101 Ranch Wild West Show, Lucille proved the critical connection for women to break into rodeo. Her greatest contribution to rodeo was steer roping, but she also entertained with exhibiting rope tricks and training horses like Governor and Tinkle, which learned tricks that classified them as "high school horses" and whom she displayed in Wild West shows, rodeo and her vaudeville act. Lucille's skill and popularity made her one of the most important Oklahoma women for early rodeo.

The Wild West show was an important gateway for western women on the public stage, particularly in exhibiting masculine skills like shooting or riding astride and, later, riding exhibition bucking horses. Important to this era was May Lillie, who became known as the "Princess of the Prairie," the "World's Champion Woman rifle shot" and the "New Rifle Queen."[61] She toured with Pawnee Bill's show and certainly influenced public opinion about western women and the West in general, as her family became important conservators of western life as some of the first buffalo preservationists in Oklahoma. By 1906, they had the "third-largest

Lucille Mulhall, circa 1905. *Photograph by Murillo Studio, St. Louis, Missouri, c1905, Rose Strothman collection. Courtesy of the Oklahoma Historical Society, 17778.*

privately owned" herd in the United States.[62] Also important in shows were twin sisters Juanita and Etheyle Parry. Their talents stood out as they performed trick riding that often led to them being referred to as Cossacks because the tricks were so dangerous. They performed for Oklahoma's 101 Ranch show. Although women ranchers had been riding astride and doing "men's work" on ranches across the territories for a long time, at a point when it was not nationally acceptable for women to participate in masculine activities, sharpshooters like Lillie and trick riders like the Parrys made it more tolerable for women to do so in public. Such women were suitable actors for introducing western women to public audiences because they remained feminine even in their masculine roles. Lucille Mulhall took such activities one step further by crossing another line viewed as unsatisfactory for women to participate in: athletic competition. Still, she, too, remained quite feminine, always wearing a long split skirt in all rodeo events when she competed.

This working cowgirl would naturally have an interest in roping contests. These rare talents, so out of context for the times that prohibited women across the United States and outside of rural ranching from participating in masculine activities, were of interest to audiences who were first introduced publicly to western women in Wild West shows. Wild West show women played a scripted role, portraying pioneering settlers. This role later expanded to include women bronc riders who exhibited their skills rather than competed for prize money. There were women who performed in Wild West shows before Lucille made her public debut, but these entertainers were advertised as daring western women or sometimes as vaqueras; they were not listed as cowgirls in the shows. While women in Wild West shows played a role in introducing women in atypical activities, it was Lucille who opened the door for women to compete in rodeo.

Lucille was born in St. Louis, Missouri, on October 21, 1885. Her father, Zack Mulhall, was a livestock purchasing agent for the Santa Fe Railroad and made the land run of 1889 to stake a claim and start a ranch near what would become Mulhall, Oklahoma, just north of the territorial capital of Guthrie in what is now Logan County.[63] Riding at an early age and roping by age four, Lucille was a natural. Her father encouraged her to rope, even saying that she could start her own herd with any strays she found, provided she could rope and brand them. Lucille created her own brand with her saddle cinch buckle, and much to her father's surprise, she soon had a bunch of yearlings from his best stock.[64] Her father recognized her talent and promoted her skills publicly at roping contests, where he bet money she

Etheyle and Juanita Parry at the 101 Ranch. *101 Ranch Collection. GM 4327.9038. Gilcrease Museum Archives.*

could out-rope the cowboys, which she did—a skill that eventually made her one of the most recognized cowgirls from Oklahoma.

Unlike many women who ranched in the West and were required to work any ranch job necessary to make the ranch a success, Lucille's family was wealthy enough to pay cowhands, so her work was optional and not a condition to feed the family. Nevertheless, she could and did "build fences, or cut the calves out of the herd and brand them." She also rode freely on the range and "took care of the cattle like a man, [kept] a count on them and had a definite answer for every detail pertaining to the ranch."[65] Even at school, she had a reputation as a good cowhand. Lucille received most of her education at St. Joseph's Convent in Guthrie, where she lived during the week, and then she returned home to the ranch on the weekends. Even at the convent, Lucille's skills were recognized, and she was called upon to help deliver a calf when one of the cows in the convent's herd was having trouble with the delivery.[66]

Lucille's various jobs on the ranch included riding roughstock. "She rode the rough-stock as routinely as any cowboy on the spread, even trying out an old longhorn or two."[67] Although all the Mulhall children, natural and adopted, could ride, the two who stood out for their mastery of it from an early age were Lucille and Charley. They often received compliments from the cowhands who worked on the ranch, and their reputation extended to

Guthrie and the surrounding areas, as the mayor sometimes requested the children to come to Guthrie to entertain visitors to the city.

Their notoriety, in part, inspired their father, then known as Colonel Mulhall, to organize a troupe called the Congress of Rough Riders and Ropers in a combination Wild West show/roundup contest. Zack's first endeavors at a show included more ranch contesting activities and less melodrama than scripted Wild West shows, which told the story of conquest in the West. His show included "horsemanship, riding, and roping" that involved actual "championships for steer roping, steer riding, saddle bronc riding, trick and fancy riding and roping."[68] Unlike the "cowboys" of Wild West shows who were contracted to act the part, most in the Mulhall troupe actually worked on ranches.[69] This type of contest, then open to top cowhands across the West, evolved into a "Contest for World's Supremecy [sic] of Rough Riders and Ropers" and gained popularity relatively quickly.[70]

In 1899, when Lucille was thirteen years old, the family began to travel, first to Krebs Park in South McAlester, Indian Territory, where she won the prize money of $1,000. She won for the best time roping and tying three steers (forty-three seconds; one minute and eleven seconds; and thirty seconds).[71] Later that year, the troupe was invited to perform at the fair in St. Louis.[72] At this time, Will Rogers joined the Mulhalls' troupe. Rogers stated, "Lucille was just a little kid when we were in St. Louis that year, but she was riding and running her Pony all over the place, and that was incidentally her start too. It was not only her start, but it was the direct start of what has since come to be known as the Cowgirl."[73] From then on, headlines about the Congress of Rough Riders and Ropers' events included the Mulhall children, with Lucille getting top billing.

It seems a nod to Teddy Roosevelt is due for helping draw national attention to ranch life in Oklahoma, but it was really his interest in Lucille's talent that landed the Oklahoma troupes in Washington, D.C. In 1900, the Mulhalls' lives changed when then vice presidential candidate Roosevelt traveled to Oklahoma Territory on his way to a Rough Riders convention in Oklahoma City. There, he attended a Fourth of July event, the "Cowboy Tournament," at the fairgrounds. More than twenty-five thousand people attended and watched Mulhall's riders and ropers and the star, fifteen-year-old Lucille. This event took place on July 3, with the full program printed in the *Oklahoma State Capital* newspaper. The agenda listed the order of events, beginning with the parade and route, followed by speeches, contests and entertainment. Only a few select people are listed in the program (in the order in which they appear): the "singing of 'The Star-Spangled Banner,' by Mme. Helena accompanied by the military band," the welcome to the Oklahoma Territory address by "Governor C.M. Barnes," the welcome to the city address by "Mayor Lee Van Winkle," an address by "Governor Theodore Roosevelt" and, for the afternoon roping and riding tournament, the only person named in the program, "Miss L. Mulhall tieing [sic] and throwing a steer."[74] After the event, Roosevelt was invited back to the Mulhall ranch. Roosevelt was so impressed that the Mulhalls and the 101 Wild West Show (of which they were now a part) were invited to perform at the McKinley-Roosevelt inaugural parade.[75] It was Roosevelt who, before leaving the ranch and Oklahoma, encouraged Zack to let the world see how great Lucille was by putting her on a stage before she "dies or gets married," leading her father to do just that.[76]

Lucille soon became known as the "original cowgirl." Along the way, she gained many other titles as newspapers and audiences grew completely enamored with her. She was described as "the most fearless and famous roper and rider in the world...the Champion Beskirted Broncho Buster, the greatest female Conqueror of Hoofs [sic], Hides, and Horns; the most famous Lassoer in Lingerie; the Rarest Rough Rider and Roper in Ribbons and Ruches." Attention to rodeo-type events and curiosity about Lucille increased as she traveled and her fame spread, and perhaps justifiably so, as she performed outstanding feats such as the 1901 horse show in Des Moines, Iowa, where she was a "sensation...[for roping] five horses simultaneously."[77] Reportedly, she could rope as many as eight horses together.

In 1901, Lucille competed at the San Angelo Fairgrounds. She was to rope last. All day the cowboys had battled the wind, which resulted in their roping times being longer than usual. The steers used were also larger than most, and Lucille broke the first rope. Regrouping to throw a second, she caught the steer and tied it in a time of twenty-nine and a half seconds, the best time of the day. She won $1,000.[78] In 1902, at the age of seventeen, she won the roping at the Cattlemen's Convention in Fort Worth, Texas. The grand prize was a $1,000 diamond championship medal for roping and tying a steer. The Fort Worth Stockman's Association was so impressed that it gave her a new nickname: "Queen of the West." Newspapers used an alternate version, calling her "Queen of the Range." In 1902, she was supposed to rope in San Antonio but had broken her leg and had to be in a wheelchair. But she was so well liked, so as not to disappoint fans who had hoped to see the headliner, organizers built a special stand so she could receive a diamond-studded medal with the Lone Star seal in the center.

At the Oklahoma City Cattlemen's Convention and in El Paso, Lucille competed in steer roping, where again she beat the men. In Dennison, Texas, in 1903, she won $1,000 for the best time out of three steers against thirty other ropers, gaining more notoriety with each victory. Audiences surprised that a petite girl could not only rope and tie a steer but did so against the men were even more impressed to find her calm and collected when mishaps occurred, like the instance in 1904 in Wichita, Kansas. Lucille overcame a major obstacle to rope her steer when he jumped a "five-foot fence" and she had to chase him down.[79]

Lucille was also well known as a horse trainer. When the Mulhalls were in New York in 1904, the *New York Times* reported about her small pony named Sambo. Lucille had trained Sambo to lead the parade without a rider to guide him, which worked until the troupe reached Central Park. There, the marchers were stopped by a mounted policeman, who informed them that "riderless horses were not permitted under any circumstances," at which point a cowboy got on Sambo and they proceeded.[80] Among her more well-known trained horses were Sam, her primary roping horse; Governor; and Tinkle, who could sit, kneel and play dead on command.[81] These anecdotal stories made major newspapers and increased her status so that by 1905, when she competed at Madison Square Garden in New York, she earned the "$5,000 Vanderbilt Club Medal for being the Greatest Horsewoman in America," as fans and competitors alike admired her skills.[82]

One of the largest and most publicized events in Oklahoma was the National Editorial Association roundup in 1905. Hosted by the 101 Miller brothers, this was a major production, with newspaper editors from across the country gathering to meet in Guthrie for a three-day convention. The Miller brothers organized a major event at the ranch in Bliss and selected Lucille to be the featured performer. She was a logical choice, being nationally recognized from the "Twin Territories to New York City as the original cowgirl." Newspapers like the *New York Times* reported sensational descriptions of her, such as that she weighed "less than a pair of fancy Mexican saddles....Lucille not only threw steers and busted broncs but also stalked prairie wolves, branded cattle, and roped as many as eight running range horses at once. She was an absolute showstopper."[83] But Oklahoma had been changing and growing, and not everyone embraced ranching or saw it as having a role in Oklahoma's future. There was concern that the Miller brothers were "projecting a hackneyed image" of Oklahoma and that such an image might detract from potential growth and progress, resulting

Lucille Mulhall and E.M. Ward, 1905. *Cabinet card. Robert G. McCubbin Western Photographs, Dickinson Research Center, National Cowboy & Western Heritage Museum. RC2019.001.064.01.*

in pushback against the Millers' plans. Nevertheless, the Millers held their ground. The *Lawton State Democrat* editors also defended against the attacks on the Millers and Lucille:

> *Some Oklahoma editors are having all kinds of spasms because Miss Mulhall, an Oklahoma girl, is going to astonish those sedate and painfully dignified people of the East with a demonstration of what she can do in the way of riding a bucking bronco and roping and tying a steer....Those editors are quaking with fear that the goggle-eyed, bean-eating, blue-bellied, codfish aristocracy of the East will be shocked into forming a mistaken idea of Oklahoma and her inhabitants....Well, here's one newspaper that is going to stand up for Miss Mulhall. She is an Oklahoma girl, an Oklahoma product, and we don't give three whoops in Hades whether those knock-kneed dudes and spindle-shanked dudesses of the East like it or not. We are ready to risk a stick of reds upon the proposition that the East can't trot out a girl that can duplicate the riding and roping of the Oklahoma Girl. Go it, Miss Mulhall, and show them there are no flies on an Oklahoma Girl.*[84]

Perhaps this description made the point of concerned officials or foreshadowed the future of Oklahoma that has grown by embracing her ranch and rodeo background. But on this occasion, it proved a positive turning point for Oklahoma.

As a woman who took her ranching skills public, Lucille stood out because of her unique abilities, gaining national publicity. It is from her competitions and beating the men at roping that she won fame. To sustain her rodeo career, Lucille would work off-season jobs. One such gig was a family affair, with her brother Charley, sister Mildred, adopted sister (also her father's mistress and biological mother to Charley and Mildred) Georgia and Lucille's husband, Martin Van Bergen (the Cowboy Baritone Vocalist), participating in the show, but it was billed as "Lucille Mulhall and her Ranch Boys."[85]

Lucille also carried her skills to the vaudeville stage. She created her own show using an act with "6 head of horses and a big Texas steer" and displayed her skills in small theaters across the United States. Insistent that the show be affordable, she ensured that prices be set "in reach of all."[86] Many vaudeville acts had reputations for just repeating the same act over and over in different cities. But newspapers made note that Lucille's show did not become mundane, stating that "such is not the case with the appearance of the girl ranger and her company in vaudeville." Her show promoted the ranching lifestyle in Oklahoma and across the United States.[87]

The written stage play *The Girl Ranger Act* starred Lucille as the girl ranger to highlight her roping and horse skills. In 1910, she formed Lucille Mulhall & Company, which performed vaudeville with a show titled Lucille Mulhall and Her Westerners.[88] Her company included Homer Wilson (later her rodeo production partner) as stage manager, brother Charley as "conductor, Walter Robbins was Train Master, and Georgia [sister] served as Secretary-Treasurer."[89] Lucille promoted the western way of life on stage and even advertised that she could "ensure the success of any fair, carnival, or other event. In addition to her roping exhibitions, she offered varied entertainment featuring any number of cattle, cowboys, cowgirls, and Indians."[90] Because her preference was to compete, she scheduled performances around the contests. "In 1915, Mulhall arranged to play the vaudeville theater in Cheyenne during the Frontier Days celebration, where she competed during the day and performed at night. Often, she simply took leave from her shows to participate in the contests, having some family member take her place."[91] Playing vaudeville from 1914 to 1916 and touring the United States and Canada, Lucille Mulhall, through her Wild West show and *The Girl Ranger Act*, re-created western life with fancy riding, rope tricks and bucking horses.

Lucille Mulhall. *Photo by Murillo Studios, St. Louis, Missouri, Rose Strothman collection, courtesy of the Oklahoma Historical Society, 17777.*

True-to-life cowboys and cowgirls rather than actors may have contributed to the success of her shows from 1900 to 1915. Lucille's fame as the "No. 1 glamour girl [promoted her more] than any other Oklahoman in history," further increasing international awareness of her as "America's First Cowgirl."[92] Her stardom from competition in the arena left many hoping to challenge her skills.

The Calgary Stampede formed in 1912 as an invitational rodeo, with solicitations extended only to the best in the world. As a special attraction, the Stampede that year advertised Lucille as the challenger to local favorite and Stampede organizer Guy Weadick's wife, Flores LaDue. The *Calgary Herald* read, "Defending World's Champion" and focused much attention on Lucille and Flores, recounting that the contest between

> *Mulhall and LaDue was very close and thrilled audiences and reporters alike. Mulhall "won repeated applause by her graceful and smooth handling of the twirling loop, and by her roping of a rider by flipping the rope with her foot," nevertheless, LaDue won the trick and fancy roping contest by tying a "double hitch in her slack rope with just two wrist movements."*[93]

Lucille and LaDue were both known across the United States and Canada, and by accepting the challenge, they brought international attention to women in rodeo, helping to promotion the newly formed Calgary Stampede, which is still a major transnational rodeo event today.

Cowgirls were substantially covered in the media even when rodeos financially failed. Fascination with professional cowgirls remained sound, and stories about individual cowgirls continued to run. At the 1913 Winnipeg Stampede, Lucille drew significant attention for steer roping when reporters learned that a cowgirl had entered the contest and would compete not in a ladies' class but against the cowboys. Although she caught and tied her steer with a respectable time of "53.35 seconds" and a cowboy won the steer roping, Lucille did not walk away empty handed, as she was named "Champion Lady Steer Roper of the World," a title she was very proud of.[94]

By 1914, as Lucille enjoyed a "National Reputation as the World's Greatest Horse Woman" and had just returned from a world tour, Oklahoma citizens were hosting a celebration in her honor.[95] By 1915, Lucille's attendance at any show or rodeo seemed to factor into the crowd turnout, like at the state fair in Sioux City, Iowa, which broke attendance records. In 1913 and 1914, crowds of 18,000 attended, but in 1915,

"Lucile [*sic*] Mulhall Lady Champion Roper, Walla-Walla Frontier Days, 1914." *Edward F. Marcell, 1914, photographic postcard. Photographic Study Collection, Dickinson Research Center, National Cowboy & Western Heritage Museum. 2005.195.*

"75,000 paid admission," lending credibility to the claim that she could guarantee a rodeo's success.[96]

With a successful Wild West show, vaudeville show and as a rodeo star, she formed her own rodeo company in 1916. This company, titled Lucille Mulhall's Round-Up, became a crucial point in cowgirl history, as she was the only female rodeo producer at that time and she also established a number of new rodeos that offered competition and employment for women. Star status, however, did not change Lucille as a person, particularly as she remained a working cowgirl. She worked the rodeo by filling in to do less than glamorous jobs, including running stock. Other cowgirls reported her to be kind and helpful even as they competed against her. In addition to roping, Lucille also worked as a pickup man and hazer, often working wherever needed to make the rodeo or show happen, even when it was in her own show or a rodeo mismanaged by someone else.

Plagued with bloomers (producers who would schedule a rodeo, take in ticket money and then run off with the money before the rodeo ended and cowboys or cowgirls were paid), rodeo struggled in the 1910s as these conditions often left the contestants and employees stranded. In 1916, after a rough year of bloomers and failed shows, like Buffalo Bill's Chicago Shan Kive, Mulhall attempted to offset the poor publicity by working the shows that had smaller purses than promised. She worked "snubbing broncs, hazing for the bulldoggers, and taking third in the cowboy steer roping." She hired many of the contestants afterward for another "eleven performances at the Milwaukee State Fair a successful endeavor that drew more than 10,000 spectators....In October, Lucille's group moved on to the American Royal Horse Show and Frontier Contest at Kansas City" before it disbanded.[97]

In 1916, Lucille Mulhall's Round-Up at the Fort Worth Stock Show "offered bronc riding, bulldogging, and steer riding and roping." By 1917, Lucille not only starred in the show as the "Fantastic Oklahoma Miss" and "champion steer roper" but also exhibited for the livestock show. Her famous steer, advertised as the "largest steer in the world," reportedly "stood over sixteen hands high and weighed more than 3,000 pounds."[98] The crowds in 1917 were the largest to that point, with "25,000 visitors... on Fort Worth Day."[99] The show that year was such a success that officials reported it was "obviously associated with the stunning performance given by the Mulhall troupe," and the directors immediately began planning to include a "contest roundup" with entry fees and cash prizes of "$3,000" that would become an annual event.[100] Lucille made history again by producing the first indoor rodeo, which opened to an estimated 23,000 people the first day, breaking another record.[101]

Regardless of where Lucille's travels led her, she always remained true to her roots, and the feeling seemed to be mutual, as she was welcomed home by organizations like the Mulhall Commercial Club. Often this included Lucille as the star entertainment, participating in a parade or sometimes a full show with her

*band of broncho busters, trick riders, and lariat spinners and gave the people of Mulhall an afternoon of recall enjoyment and fun....Miss Mulhall herself rode her educated horse, who has almost human intelligence. She also did some lariat spinning and trick roping. Using an 80-foot rope, she captured from three to five horses at one throw.*[102]

In her many travels, she never forgot home and always appreciated it. Lucille continued to promote ranching life and rodeo into her fifties. In 1934, at the second annual Knox-Mulhall Rodeo, she performed her last roping exhibition. The following year would be her last public appearance, riding in the parade at the Eighty-Niners' Day Rodeo at Guthrie, Oklahoma. She said it would be her last attendance, although she planned to keep riding horses, stating she would do so "as long as I can get a leg across." She only

Ruth Roach, Fox Hastings and Bea Kirnan in 1928 at the Sioux City RoundUp. *101 Ranch Collection, GM 4327.8544. Gilcrease Museum Archives.*

had five more years to enjoy horseback riding before she was killed in an auto accident in 1940.[103]

Her greatest contribution to rodeo was in creating an opening for women to compete. Where later in rodeo history women's participation in roughstock and other events would come into question, Lucille created opportunity in the arena for women at a time when their involvement in rodeo helped bring it to the international stage. Cowgirls reported her as being helpful even in competition. Ruth Roach considered her "not only a role model but a personal mentor and friend."[104] Lucille's genuine love for rodeo and ranching was evident in her willingness to make it a success, even from behind the spotlight. She created the opening for women professionally in rodeo, competing in the same events the men did for forty years and leaving rodeo history to be written in part by Oklahoma cowgirls.

# Chapter 3

# FIRSTS, TRENDSETTERS AND RECORD BREAKERS

There were many firsts and records in rodeo achieved by and because of women in Oklahoma. From Lucille Mulhall being America's First Cowgirl and internationally known female steer roper to Alice Adams Holden, who was the first woman to win bronc riding against the men at the rodeo in Fort Worth, Texas, a pioneering spirit embodies the women of Oklahoma who led the field in many ways.

Several issues plagued early rodeo, notably significant expenses for contestants traveling (many with their own bucking horses) before the railroads partnered with larger rodeos. Also, mismanagement often left rodeo producers broke, and bloomers left contestants stranded with no salary. The first efforts to help correct these issues began with the Wild Bunch Cowboy Association (WBCA), which was formed in 1915 by Lucille Mulhall and business partner Homer Wilson. This organization tried to make events fairer for competitors by standardizing rules. Lucille implemented into her rodeo productions changes that required consistency in roping for contestants and improved conditions for livestock. For example, at the Muskogee Roundup in April 1915, Lucille tackled problems concerning the "endangerment of cattle as her production integrated rules endorsed by the WBCA to lessen the chance of injury to steers in the steer roping. 'The rules were clean head, half head, or both horns catch. Crosstie three feet and each roper allowed two loops, cattle given 60 feet start and a ten-foot foul line with a ten-second fine if disqualified.'"[105] This made clear rules for roping and also reduced the number of injured stock or loss of steers. Although the WBCA did not last, it was an important start toward standardizing rodeo. Lucille also worked toward improving opportunities for contestants, particularly cowgirls.

As the first female rodeo producer in 1917, Lucille Mulhall extended more jobs to cowgirls in her productions and added rodeos in new areas where there were none previously. As the most well-known cowgirl throughout the business, and with a reputation that she could guarantee the success of any show, she combined her reputation with innovative ideas to promote rodeo. That same year, she produced a successful roundup in San Antonio, Texas, where she and Wilson implemented a new marketing strategy distributing "souvenir steer-head pins" that were sold throughout the Greater San Antonio area by cooperating businesses. The result was advanced sales for the rodeo and additional generated business for the local merchants who took part. These pins entitled the wearer to free admission to the roundup on rodeo day, but as people bought and wore them around town, they increased community awareness about the rodeo and provided a type of free advertising. This is a marketing technique still used by some stock shows today. The San Antonio rodeo was also a venue open to changing roughstock procedures.

Lucille's rodeo dramatically changed roughstock competition by being the first to use enclosed chutes to hold the bucking horses or bulls. These first chutes used at the San Antonio roundup replaced the earlier method of earing down a bronc in the open or blindfolding the animal while a rider mounted. The chute could hold the animal in place for the rider and prevent any mishaps if a snubber dropped an ear or a horse reared in resistance. Within two years, other large rodeos like Cheyenne also began to use chutes.[106] As Lucille continued to compete and other women joined rodeo, more crowds noticed.

Women attracted audiences who were curious to see cowgirls compete but found that they were wowed by their abilities. Cowgirls set many record firsts—some quite spectacular. Mildred Douglas from Lawton, Oklahoma, is known as the world's first woman steer rider. Some cowgirls rode broncs that men had failed to ride or that were known to be extra rank. Mildred was also the first cowgirl to ride the "famous Two Step" bucking horse.[107] Mildred was a trick rider and shooter and worked for the 101 Ranch and in the 101 Wild West show. In 1918, she rode in Tucumcari Roundup in Tucumcari, New Mexico. Bronc horses can be particularly tough, and although some contractors kept a separate string for cowgirls to ride, many did not, leaving most girls to ride whatever they drew. Cowgirls then sometimes rode the same bucking horses as the cowboys, even those with reputations as killer broncs. Mildred drew a tough bronc at Tucumcari described as a "head fighter, and [it was] just three or four jumps before the whistle [when] the horse jerked the rein out of Mildred's hand but quick as a flash she threw both hands in the air and she rode the bucker to the finish without a rein. To the judges it looked like she had deliberately thrown the rein away so that she could prove her riding ability, and they awarded her first prize," making her one of the only known cowgirls to win without reins.[108]

The first woman to beat the men in Roman races at the Calgary Stampede was Florence Holmes from Ardmore. Florence is in many rodeo programs under various names (Florence Hughes, Florence King and Florence Fenton) until she married cowboy Floyd Randolph in 1925, and from then on, she went by Florence Randolph.[109] She first entered the Roman standing race at the 1919 Calgary Stampede and won, beating out fourteen men and earning her credit as the "only woman to ever accomplish such a feat."[110] She won a saddle valued at $1,500 and a trophy. In her rodeo career, she competed in ladies' bronc riding, trick riding and Roman standing races. She also was one of the many cowgirls who worked in Hollywood in between rodeo seasons, using the additional part-time job to help support her rodeo career. In Hollywood, she worked as a stuntwoman, reportedly earning as much as "two or three hundred dollars for a five minute ride." Such pay influenced her decision to stay a month longer than planned.[111] This, too, influenced Hollywood, which recruited rodeo folks to work with horses and for stunts, which in turn also helped publicize rodeo.

"Mildred Douglas at rodeo in Garden City, Kansas, 1917." #114 Mildred Chrisman Collection, Museum of the Great Plains, Lawton, Oklahoma.

"Mildred Douglas winning championship lady bucking horse riding at Dewey Roundup on 'Nigger Baby,' Sept 1916, Kansas City, Missouri. Horse belonged to Joe Bartles (the city of Bartlesville is named after him.)." *#113 Mildred Chrisman Collection, Museum of the Great Plains, Lawton, Oklahoma.*

A cowgirl who had one of the longer careers in rodeo and was a favorite among fans was Pauline Nesbitt of Nowata, Oklahoma. Nesbitt was a bronc rider and trick rider who rodeoed from 1922 until 1948.[112] She made her own costumes, which led to her being a "model along with three other rodeo cowgirls in the 1941 Sears and Roebuck Catalog."[113] This side job for Sears placed the image of real cowgirls in homes across the United States. Pauline stayed involved in the ranch-rodeo life after her rodeo career by ranching and raising cattle and horses.

As rodeo evolved and divided, women both contributed to and benefited from some changes. One change was the professionalization of barrel racing. The first rodeo association to recognize this event as a "world championship event" and the first to create "a Board of Governors including representatives from each segment of rodeo—stock contractors, contestants, fans, producers, and contract performers" was the International Rodeo Association (IRA).[114] In 1946, the Rodeo Association of America merged with the National Rodeo Association to form the International Rodeo Association, which oversaw rodeos in Oklahoma, Texas and New Mexico.[115] The IRA allowed contestants to enter regardless of their membership in what was then called the RCA, or Rodeo Cowboys Association (the predecessor of the Professional Cowboy Rodeo Association or PRCA). The RCA often blacklisted contestants who violated its rules or bylaws, including a rule prohibiting members from joining multiple professional organizations. As part of its marketing strategy, the IRA "created the position of Miss Rodeo America as an ambassador for the entire sport, to travel around the country appearing on television and radio and making public appearances to promote local rodeos."[116] By this point, women supported and promoted rodeo in many ways.

Although women had been riding broncs for some time, Alice Adams Holden from Bluejacket, Oklahoma, was the first woman to win bronc riding against the men at the rodeo in Fort Worth, Texas. Promotional materials for this rodeo did not list "cowgirls' bronc riding contest," so Alice talked to the officials, as there were no other "cowgirl bronc riders there." She planned to ride for a "twenty-five dollar fee," although she would get paid only if she rode. "Alice drew the toughest bucker of the entire string, a horse

Pauline Nesbitt (*seated*) in New York with other girls. *Photographer unknown, 1914, gelatin silver print. Rodeo Photographs, Dickinson Research Center, National Cowboy & Western Heritage Museum. 88.9.1287.*

called 'Red Rambler' well known to the horsemen and rodeo fans" as a killer bronc. Alice rode the bronc, and the announcer stated that "first prize was fifty dollars," which was twice as much as she would have earned as a contracted employee riding an exhibition ride. She earned the fifty dollars because she beat the cowboys in their own men's division.[117] Alice earned a PRCA Gold Card, and she and her husband, Pete, helped standardize rodeo in Oklahoma by specializing the program, speeding up events and adding glamour to the rodeos they produced.

Of the firsts, rarities like Lucyle Richards—who might be the first and only woman bucked off a bronc to land on a pickup man's shoulders when dismounting—certainly stand out. Lucyle was born in Pushmataha County, Oklahoma, and took part in her first rodeo when she was thirteen years old in Talihina, Oklahoma, where she rode bucking steers and horses. Through the 1920s and 1930s, she toured with Adams Rodeo and Wild West show, Jack King's Wild West show, Bob McKinley's Wild West show and the 101 Wild West shows. She rode broncs and did trick riding, specializing in shoulder stands, slick stands, tall stands, cartwheels, crouper rollups and back drags. She won numerous world championships as a saddle bronc rider over her

Alice Adams riding Yellow Fever at the King Bro's. Rodeo, 1927, Columbia, South Carolina. *Photographer unknown, 1927, gelatin silver print. Rodeo Photographs, Dickinson Research Center, National Cowboy & Western Heritage Museum. 88.9.1338.*

Lucyle Richards on White Lightning. *Photographer unknown, date unknown, gelatin silver print. Rodeo Photographs, Dickinson Research Center, National Cowboy & Western Heritage Museum. 88.9.1383.*

career, including in Chicago in 1930, in Boston in 1934 and at a Girls Rodeo Association (GRA) rodeo in Oklahoma City in 1951.

Again, reiterating that rodeo is often a family affair, contestants can vary greatly by age. Many children follow their parents into rodeo and acquire skills for it at an early age; most of them have grown up on ranches and come into rodeo naturally. Occasionally, young athletes rise to the height of their careers at an early age. One phenomenal example is Ann Lewis.

Ann was born in Sulphur, Oklahoma, and started barrel racing in kindergarten. At eight years old, she was the youngest member of the IPRA. Nicknamed "Annie the Oakie," in 1968 at the Houston rodeo, Ann rode in the Astrodome in front of forty-five thousand people. She won $1,064, one of the largest checks in rodeo at that time.[118] She became the youngest girl to win (albeit posthumously) the National Finals Rodeo world championship in barrel racing. Ann had the title going into the Finals, with winnings totaling $8,928, and due to the rule that ranked winners based on total annual

Ann Lewis or "Annie the Oakie." *Photographer unknown, date unknown, gelatin silver print. Rodeo Photographs, Dickinson Research Center, National Cowboy & Western Heritage Museum, Oklahoma City, Oklahoma. 88.9.1352.*

earnings, she was able to keep the lead even without being there. Ann did not make it to the Finals rodeo due to a tragic wreck that took her life in 1967. Also killed in the wreck were Ann's twin sister, Jan; her mother, Rose; and Sissy Thurman, a nine-time world champion qualifier who was in third

Ann Lewis, the youngest girl to win the National Finals Rodeo world championship in barrel racing. *Photographer unknown, date unknown, gelatin silver print. Rodeo Photographs, Dickinson Research Center, National Cowboy & Western Heritage Museum. 88.9.1353.*

place for the Finals that year and was sharing a ride with the Lewis family to the Finals. This combined loss took a tremendous toll on the entire rodeo community.[119] Ann, however, had started a trend of Oklahoma cowgirls holding consecutive titles of world champion barrel racers that lasted from 1968 to 1974.[120] Ann won in 1968, followed by Missy Long from Duncan in 1969; Joyce Burk, also from Duncan, in 1970; Donna Patterson from Tecumseh in 1971; Gail Petska from Tecumseh, who won back to back in 1972 and 1973; and, in 1974, Jeana Day Felts from Woodward.

Continuing an outstanding streak for barrel racers, the first Oklahoma cowgirl to break the record for qualifying for the National Finals the most times in one event was Sherry Combs-Johnson from Addington, Oklahoma. Sherry qualified for the Finals rodeo consecutively from 1959 to 1968, again in 1970 and in 1991.[121] Barrel racing flourished in Oklahoma, both producing winning athletes and organizing and improving the event.

The first cowgirl to make the cover of *Rodeo Sport News* was Carol Gurley Goostree from Verden, Oklahoma. She was an officer in the Oklahoma Barrel Racing Association in 1974. Carol trained five horses that made it to the NFR, and she won championships at the GRA in 1978, the WPRA in 1979 and the NFR from 1978 to 1980.

Whether it be preserving heritage or sustaining family, women were at the forefront of community and rodeo support, building rodeo into what it is today. The Rodeo in Ada, Oklahoma, provides a good example of how community, and specifically women in local areas, added to the overall preservation of ranching heritage and rodeo. The Big Ada Round-up and Frontier Days began in 1921, when out-of-town promoters asked the local American Legion post about staging a rodeo. Although the Legionnaires were on board, the women of the town's Mother's Club, led by President Mrs. Tom Hope, objected—not to the rodeo itself, but to out-of-towners hosting it. Convincing the Legionnaires to promote the rodeo locally, the first rodeo was held on June 16–18, 1921.[122] By 1935, the management and production responsibilities transferred to the Ada Fire Department, and it became known as the Ada Fireman's Rodeo. The date the rodeo was held moved to August, and the committee added a jackpot of $500 in prize money and advertised famous contestants Dick Truitt and cowgirls Grace and Vivian White from Ringwood, Oklahoma, as well as Josephine Proctor from Okemah, Oklahoma, resulting in crowds of thirty-eight thousand in a two-day period.[123]

These achievements could not have been possible without the leadership, participation and support of women like Nell Truitt Shaw. The rodeo remained popular through the Depression, but World War II placed additional responsibilities on the fire department, and in 1942, sponsorship of the rodeo changed to the Ada Round-Up Club and the Junior Chamber of Commerce. In 1949, the Elks Club began sponsoring the rodeo, and it became so popular that the following year, it exceeded Cheyenne in attendance and prize money.[124] This began a period of success, and by 1955, the best contestants in the country were adding Ada to their schedule of rodeos. In 1958, it was "ranked 5th in the United States by the RCA."[125] Nell grew up near Stonewall, Oklahoma, where her father was a livestock inspector and her brothers rodeoed. Through her brother Dick's rodeo career, Nell met and married Everett Shaw. It was during this period of success in Ada that Everett and Nell met Ken and Ruth Lance, who together were involved in the rodeo becoming professionally sanctioned. Nell sold tickets, put up posters and worked wherever necessary during the rodeo. She continued to work with the Lances at the rodeo until 1990.[126]

Where cowgirl contestants were often born into ranch and rodeo families, still others married into the life. Cleo Crouch Rude grew up near Doby Springs, ten miles west of Buffalo, Oklahoma. There she helped her father, George Cleo, with ranch work and to put on rodeos at the ranch.[127] It was a natural transition, then, when she married Ike Rude in November 1937 and they immediately began rodeoing right after the wedding.[128] Attending rodeos with their husbands, women perform various jobs, such as being grooms, secretaries and laundresses, just to name a few. But of these three, anything relating to the animals would be priority. At the Treasure Island Rodeo in San Francisco in 1939, wives rode in the parade in place of the cowboys because contestants were required to ride in grand entries and parades at most rodeos.[129] Having their wives fill in could prevent a cowboy from being disqualified.

Clem McSpadden, responsible for so many improvements to the National Finals Rodeo while it was held in Oklahoma, was a well-known rodeo announcer. He shined in rodeo but also served his community. His wife, Donna Casity McSpadden, traveled to rodeos with her husband, recalling that life on the road was an adventure but it was also what made rodeo a family. Sometimes they were too close for comfort when cowboys roomed with them and others stopped in for food and a shower. Donna recalled, "They knew I always kept sandwich fixings and snacks in the room. I don't know how many times one of the guys needed to shower and use the last clean towel."[130] In addition to hosting rodeo contestants, the McSpaddens also served the people of Oklahoma. Clem was in the Oklahoma State Senate for eight years and later the United States House of Representatives, and Donna worked for the Oklahoma Crime Commission Law Enforcement Assistance Administration. While Clem was general manager of the National Finals Rodeo when it was in Oklahoma City, Donna worked to preserve rodeo history by serving as president of the Rodeo Historical Society. To help rodeo families in times of need, Donna founded a group called H.A.N.D.S. (Helping A Needy Diva Survive).[131] Her other charitable endeavors supported both large organizations and local needs. The Bushyhead Art Show, which spotlighted artists specializing in western and Native American artwork, was created to raise funds for the American Heart Association and, locally, to donate money toward building the Chelsea Public Library.[132]

Women who married into rodeo or competed briefly often switched their interest to other ways of support when they stopped competing. Some organized events, charities or even fashion shows to support families of rodeo contestants. Margaret Hart Deakins helped Donna McSpadden "organize a style show in which wives of the cowboys modeled."[133] Margaret was also a member of the Rodeo Historical Society. The style show included prizes to elicit supporters. Some prizes were extravagant, like the "Frederick Remington oil painting…[and] leather saddle purse" that Margaret won one year.[134] The can-do, will-do attitude prompted these women to make rodeo successful by working in less than glamourous jobs and anywhere needed. These charitable endeavors may seem like behind-the-scenes work but have proven invaluable to the greater rodeo family in ways like the hospitality or Gold Card room for families during the NFR and in sustaining the rodeo community.

Also important is improving stock. On the early frontier, nineteenth-century ranching women had learned about breeding cattle. This tradition continues today. Linda Ament Russell is heavily involved in raising bucking bulls on the Russell ranch, where in addition to having expert knowledge about breeding history for each bull and keeping their registration records, she can also identify minute details about their care, like if a "bull is on a special diet because he has a delicate stomach."[135] Today, when rodeo stock is also ranked as champion level, this is an important part of the industry for stock contractors as well as the athletes dependent on quality animals for earning points.

Women also supported both rodeo and contestants by sometimes sacrificing their own careers, like Michelle Smith West, who grew up near Henrietta and stopped barrel racing to advance her husband, Terry Don, from Tulsa, who became a world champion. Michelle became his "business manager, travel agent," and it changed his career trajectory. In 1995, he placed second, and in 1996, he won the world championship at the National Rodeo Finals. Terry Don had another good year in 2003, qualifying for the National Finals and winning the Pace Picante Series, which he had also qualified for four times.[136] Personal reasons may explain such a gesture, but similar to women who worked early ranches to ensure their success, this history of self-sacrifice and high work ethic remains part of rodeo.

Central to the success of any rodeo is the job of rodeo secretary. Valued by contestants and other workers who recognize her importance, she is often referred to as the "'Store Keeper,' and absolute boss." The rodeo secretary might be a local volunteer or a full-time professional rodeo secretary, but a rodeo will not run smoothly without this position.[137] Jo Ramsey Decker was about thirteen when she became interested in rodeo. Graduating from high school in Sallisaw, Oklahoma, she started a journey to Madison Square Garden in New York City when she was chosen to be the ranch girl of the year. That award required her to attend the rodeo. "She won the award again in 1946 making her only one of two girls to win the honor twice."[138] When she married, her husband, H.D. Binns, was the stock contractor for the rodeo at Dewey, Oklahoma. He hired Jo as rodeo secretary. She would serve in that capacity for twenty-five years.

"Her job was to collect entry fees, type the names of all the contestants and what event they entered. All of the livestock were number[ed], and those numbers were drawn and given to a cowboy." Sometimes a rodeo secretary works inside the arena as well. "Jo often acted as a flag bearer." Most importantly, she tracked the winners by recording times or scores in each event and kept up with who placed in each go-round and the average. "She calculated all of the winnings and wrote the checks....If she had to work the slack after the main rodeo was over."[139] The rodeo does not function without this position.

Cowgirls had designed and sewn their own consumes since 1900 for practical reasons (skirts compromised safety in bronc rigging) and for style, reflecting each cowgirl's individual personality. In addition to being a rodeo secretary, Jo designed and sold western wear that became very popular. Some requests for her designs came from top stars in music and Hollywood. She received orders from "Rex Allen, Rose Maddox, Lynn Anderson, and even the late Princess Grace of Monaco special ordered Jo Decker Originals. Neiman Marcus had a special Jo Decker section in their store and often held showings for her in Dallas and Houston."[140] Jo earned a reputation in her position as rodeo secretary and in 1959 became "production coordinator" for the first National Finals Rodeo held in Dallas, where "her job was to plan the opening ceremonies for ten performances and to carry the American flag for each." Jo went on to be secretary at the National Finals Rodeo seven times.[141]

Even in retirement, Jo continued to work, serving on the local county fair board. During her tenure there, she promoted the fair, and the board not only recovered from deficit funds but also developed enough funds to erect a new county fair barn. The structure, dedicated to Jo, was named the Jo Decker County Fair Building. After years of commitment and having served on the Rodeo Historical Society Board from 1996 to 1999, Jo received the Tad Lucas Award from the National Cowboy & Western Heritage Museum for her work and dedication to rodeo. One finds evidence of her extensive involvement in rodeo through Jo having earned a gold card membership with the PRCA and other memberships with the American Quarter Horse Association, rodeo Cowboy Alumni Association and the Rodeo Historical Society.[142]

Between 1990 and 2008, 36 percent of the specialty acts voted to perform at the National Finals Rodeo were from Oklahoma; of those, 56 percent were women. From 1990 to 1998, the first woman from Oklahoma whose specialty act was selected both solo and with her husband's was Vicki

Herrera Adams from Stuart. Vicki was born and raised on the Yakama Reservation in Toppenish, Washington (enrolled Cowlitz). Growing up around rodeo, Vicki was drawn to it through family association. Influenced by her father, Bill Herrera, who was all-around rodeo champion in the Northwest Indian Rodeo Association, Vicki became interested in rodeo[143] after seeing a trick rider perform at a rodeo in Oregon. Riding by age eleven, when she got her first trick riding saddle, she learned to trick ride and competed in barrel races. She won the barrel racing championship in the Northwest Indian Rodeo Association four times, but her trick riding advanced when she met Dick and Connie Griffith at the rodeo at Ellensburg, Washington, and began to train with them during the summer. She continued to rodeo until she graduated high school and then joined the Rodeo Cowboys Association (RCA). While attending the Contract Act convention for the RCA, held in Denver, Colorado, she met her future husband, Leon Adams, from Oklahoma.[144] Inviting her to Oklahoma to train, Vicki stayed with Leon's sister and brother-in-law, where she learned Roman riding and worked on her trick riding. Six months later, Leon asked her to marry him, and in Santa Maria, California, in June 1970, they did.[145] Nominated nineteen times, her specialty act won Contract Act of the Year four times. Vicki and Leon shared rodeo and the rodeo life around the world, showing in Finland, Japan and France. Like in other rodeo legacy families, their daughter Kerri also became a rodeo performer, staying with relatives during the school year and rodeoing during the summer.[146] Vickie became so well known for her skills that she consulted and trained horses for a variety of interests or purposes. She worked for the film industry on several projects, including a documentary about Monroe Veach, the famous saddle maker. She performed stunts in the movie *Buffalo Girls* and trained horses for the movie *Horse Crazy*. Recognized nationally for her accomplishments, she has carried the American flag at the National Finals Rodeo six times. She was on the cover of *America's Horse Magazine* in 1998 for earning the Versatility Award at the American Quarter Horse Association (AQHA) Champion.[147] The National Cowboy of Color Museum and Hall of Fame honored Vicki's accomplishments by inducting her into the Hall of Fame in 2005; she is only the second woman and the first Native American woman to receive such an honor.[148] Vicki and her husband, Leon, were inducted into the ProRodeo Hall of Fame in 2008. In addition to her accolades in the arena, she is a talented horse trainer, having several horses win the honor to carry the flag at the National Finals Rodeo. She and Leon also won Conservative Rancher of the Year in 1993.[149]

For all the jobs outside the arena spotlight, from the rodeo secretary, to driver, to manager, to charity work—supporting roles women mastered with a determination similar to women who had ranched for decades—women built rodeo with their contributions and support of one another as well as the business, leading to many of the firsts that cowgirls accomplished. All these gains proved equally important during times of loss. When rodeo and the United States were enduring the dark decades of economic depression followed by world war, the women who helped keep the home fires burning also kept the arena lights on.

Chapter 4

# GETTING THROUGH
# THE HARD TIMES

**R**odeo has survived some tough times; of these, two world wars and a depression were the most impactful. However, rodeo is a community-based event, and because rodeo has always given back to the community, the sentiment has been mutually beneficial. Rodeo includes a history of hosting fundraising events to support the Red Cross or war efforts, as well as to help orphans and assist with disaster relief or needy families. The community, in turn, seems to find a way to attend rodeos even in extremely difficult circumstances. During the height of the Depression or when rationing gasoline and tires during World War II made it arduous to even get to the rodeo, people found a way.

The Depression strained rodeo as economic factors made producing rodeo more difficult. Without assured crowds to pay admission to help offset the cost of production, small rodeos suffered the most. Rodeos in cities, however, kept steady spectators. Perhaps the rodeo offered an option to people in need of escape, and rodeo was similar in cost to the motion picture industry that thrived between the 1930s and into the 1940s. Averaging audiences of "eighty-five million weekly," rodeo remained popular.[150]

Considering the times, rodeo contestants' prize monies during the Depression were good. Mary Lou LeCompte, in *Cowgirls of the Rodeo: Pioneer Professional Athletes*, states that in 1935, cowboys could earn "an estimated $2,000 per year," and by 1937, when "average income was $3,000…at least thirty top hands earned between $8,000 and $9,000."[151] Furthermore, women in rodeo also earned much higher than average salaries of other occupations for women during the Depression, with cowgirls earning as much as "$2,000 per event."[152] Part of the reason rodeo remained popular was the carryover of veteran cowgirls who became stars in the 1920s.

One memorable cowgirl who rodeoed through the rough years was Mildred Douglas Chrisman. Mildred was born in Philadelphia and attended a Connecticut boarding school "where horseback riding was part of the curriculum." Through school friends, she met Ray and Minnie Thomson, who trained horses in Bridgeport, Connecticut. "There Mildred learned to ride and jump, both English and sidesaddle."[153] From there she went to Barnum and Bailey's Circus and then got into rodeo. Mildred rode broncs and steers before she began trick riding. Her trick riding career began by chance in 1916 at the Royal American Stock Show in Kansas City, Missouri, where she got her start as a fill-in. Trick riding contests at that time were judged by skill and difficulty of the tricks. Any contests with fewer than three entries were subject to cancellation. In Kansas City, Mayme Stroud and Babe Willetts entered, and Mildred agreed to compete so the event would make. She borrowed a horse from Lucille Mulhall and won second place.[154] She was also in motion pictures, and "in 1917 she started out by playing the Tex Austin Roundup at El Paso and then on to Fort Worth for the Homer Wilson–Lucille Mulhall Rodeo in connection with the Fat Stock Show and then on the Ringling Circus for the wild west concert."[155] Among the many contests she won were those in Garden City, Kansas; Pendleton Round-Up; Denver; Cheyenne Frontier Days; and Belle Fourche Roundup. Mildred settled near Lawton and, like many, worked in town to help financially support her ranch. While keeping her ranch, Mildred also worked the WPA projects in four Oklahoma counties near Lawton, processing payroll and reviewing time sheets and paychecks for "thousands of W.P.A. workers," resulting in her being well known in rodeo and locally in Comanche County.[156]

Another popular cowgirl from the 1920s was trick rider, bronc rider, trick roper and stuntwoman Florence Randolph. Florence was thirteen when she learned to ride, and by fourteen, she had joined with Ringling Brothers Circus as an apprentice with families and to learn to trick ride. After that, she organized her own show, the Princess Mohawk's Wild West Hippodrome, employing workers who "toured the United States conducting wild west shows."[157]

Florence came to live in Oklahoma after meeting her husband, Floyd, who was a judge at the rodeo in Dewey. Rodeo continued to be part of their lives and even their honeymoon as they at once left Newkirk, Oklahoma, after the wedding ceremony in 1925 to head down the road for a rodeo the very next

"Mildred Chrisman on 'Silver King,' Lawton, ca. 1940. Taken at their first farm south of Lawton. Windows in building came from their tour bus." *#128 Mildred Chrisman Collection, Museum of the Great Plains, Lawton, Oklahoma.*

day. Because rodeo was Florence's professional career, Floyd had a practice track built for her at their home and ranch near Ardmore, Oklahoma, to match the dimensions of the arena at Madison Square Garden. There, she worked, trained horses and helped run the ranch. They helped supply stock for larger rodeos, including Madison Square Garden from 1925 to 1939. One of the more famous horses from their ranch was a trick horse named

*Above*: "Mildred Chrisman in parade, Lawton, Oklahoma; ca. 1946." *#88 Mildred Chrisman Collection, Museum of the Great Plains, Lawton, Oklahoma.*

*Right*: Florence Randolph. *Clay Dahlberg, circa 1940, safety film negative. Rodeo Photographs via Tad S. Mizwa, Dickinson Research Center, National Cowboy & Western Heritage Museum. 2005.003.3.38A.19A.*

Boy. Boy's markings included a remarkable "map of the United States on his right side" that earned notice by *Ripley's Believe It or Not!* when they were in New York. The amazing horse also went in an elevator up "16 flights" at the Bellevue-Stratford Hotel in Philadelphia to make an appearance at a Rotary Club event. He was so special that the City of Ardmore supplied a tombstone for his grave when he died at the age of thirty-five.[158] Florence was active in the community and helped produce and manage the rodeo in Ardmore. She was a "ten times World Champion Cowgirl Trick Rider and World Champion Bronc Rider," resulting in her induction into the National Cowboy Hall of Fame in 1968.[159]

Florence publicized rodeo with one of the wildest stunts, in which she rode a bucking airplane with a saddle strapped "behind the open cockpit of an old Curtiss bi-wing at Love Field in Dallas" to promote the Dallas Dunbar Rodeo. Rodeo continued during the Great Depression of the late 1920s and early 1930s, partially because cowgirls took part in raising money for relief funds that helped those in need and kept rodeo going as well. Like other rodeo cowgirls, Florence represented Oklahoma nationally and, as she became more famous, internationally. Two years in a row, 1927 and 1928, she won the Juergens and Anderson World Champion Cowgirl Trick Rider, and in 1930, she took the Champion All-Around Cowgirl at Philadelphia. When she won bronc and trick riding championships at Chicago and the World's Championship Rodeo in New York, winning the Metro-Goldwyn-Mayer $10,000 trophy (twice), even Fifth Avenue residents of New York became interested in rodeo.[160] In 1932, Florence and other cowgirls received special recognition for their charity work and their special appearances at local hospitals in New York when Mrs. William Randolph Hearst honored them at a luncheon to acknowledge their support of the charity the Milk and Ice Fund.[161] Florence also did this type of charity work at home in Ardmore, where she and Floyd sponsored a rodeo to contribute to the Oklahoman Milk and Ice Fund. The rodeo was successful and continued for several years. Many contestants and rodeos experienced hard times during the Depression, when few people were carrying cash, but programs like this brought attention to rodeo, not just for entertainment, but also for rodeo's long practice of giving back to families in the community.

Lucyle Roberts also did a great deal for rodeo in the 1930s. Lucyle lived in Antlers, Oklahoma, but her rodeo life required her to spend a great deal of time on the road. Throughout the 1920s and 1930s, she traveled extensively to compete in the United States and abroad. In 1930, she won the All-Around Cowgirl Championship of the Southwest at the Clayton,

New Mexico rodeo. She was an all-around cowgirl, winning her first championship in 1929 at Pampa, Texas, for fastest time in wrestling three steers, each weighing an average of seven hundred pounds.[162] The 1930s also took her abroad to Europe and Australia, and she competed for almost a year in Mexico. In Chihuahua and Juarez, "she pulled off one of the most daring stunts a girl could tackle, when she elected to attempt and did ride those fierce big black Spanish bulls, of the Mexican bullfight rings."[163] There, too, she and Violet Clement made the headline alongside and listed before famous cowboys: "Violet Clement y Lucile [*sic*] Roberts y los Famosos Charros José De Anda, Silviano Sanchez y Leo Murray."[164] Continuing to travel far from her Oklahoma home, she also competed in Australia in 1934, taking American rodeo global.

Starting in 1929, cowgirls began competing in calf roping, and by the 1930s, interest in the event had grown. Some rodeos hosting calf roping

Possibly Lucyle Richards in Roman riding pose, standing with one foot on each horse with hat raised. *Ralph R. Doubleday, circa 1935, nitrate negative. Ralph R. Doubleday Rodeo Photographs, Dickinson Research Center, National Cowboy & Western Heritage Museum. 79.026.2699.*

Lucyle bulldogging in Ardmore. *Photographer unknown, gelatin silver print. Rodeo Photographs, Dickinson Research Center, National Cowboy & Western Heritage Museum. 88.9.1382.*

offered significant prize money, like the 1936 rodeo in Sidney, Iowa, in which "157 women…competed for $6,000 in prizes," keeping cowgirls' star status equivalent to what it had been in the 1920s. Bigger rodeos in areas like Detroit, Philadelphia, Indianapolis, Dallas, Chicago, New York and Boston continued to be popular during the 1930s, so much so that the managers of the Boston Garden were paying an advance to have well-known producer Colonel William T. Johnson produce the rodeo there. In 1936, his advancement was "more than $80,000," indicating that larger venues were profiting from rodeo even amid the Depression.[165] Women competed, performed and were integral to advertising the rodeo, often portraying Johnson surrounded by a "bevy of cowgirls…featured in the advance publicity for his rodeos."[166] This role in advertising marks a shift in women's role in rodeo as well.

Lucyle was popular not only for her outstanding athletic abilities but also for her remarkable beauty, which seemed often to be included in headlines about her rodeoing. For example, when *New York Times* writer Sam Cohen covered the story about the upcoming Annual Championship Rodeo finals in

Boston, her name was in the headline, "Lucyle Roberts, 'Queen of Saddle,' Rides Here," but he included a subtitle commenting on her looks: "Beautiful Cowgirl Is Most Daring and Champion of Rodeos."[167] From the time the first cowgirls were headlining in newspapers, reporters often commented on their feminine qualities. Such writers were often surprised that the girls had not lost those qualities with their ability to rope a one-thousand-pound steer. In 1934, for example, in describing bronc rider Lucyle Richards, her appearance rather than her championships is highlighted, as she is described as "both the prettiest and best dressed of all the cowgirls, adding that her combination of beauty and skill had brought the Madison Square Garden crowd of 18,000 to its feet."[168]

In such trying times, many unemployed folks and anyone with the gumption to do so could enter to try to win a bronc contest. Men who were not from ranching backgrounds and not raised working alongside women doing the same ranch work as men began to enter rodeo, and this changed attitudes about women competing.[169] The cowgirls referred to them as the new cowboys. In their efforts to improve the financial inconsistences in rodeo, the men formed a new organization, and while cowgirls could be members, they did not have a vote in the newly formed Cowboy Turtle Association (CTA). One method the CTA used to force change was to strike, and while this worked to improve monies and conditions for cowboys, it marked a turning point of decline in women's athletic events.

Some smaller rodeos that struggled during the Depression reduced competition events for women. By the 1940s, women's roles had changed, as it was necessary for them to become wage earners outside the home to help fill the labor shortage left by men serving overseas. For rodeo women who had been wage earners since the 1910s, the result was a drastic change when women's competition in rodeo met with the newly created sponsor girls.

The idea for sponsor girls began in 1931 at the Stamford, Texas Cowboy Reunion. Participating in more of a beauty contest than a contest of cowgirl skill, sponsor girls (ages sixteen and up) dressed up, rode in the parade and rode a figure-eight pattern around barrels so judges could critique their skills on horseback. The girl with the highest points in three areas—her horse; her costume and attractiveness; and her riding skills—was awarded prizes funded by area businesses. Sponsor girls became part of rodeos across the Southwest, and each rodeo had some variation to make its contest unique. Some rodeos had the riding skills judged on the cloverleaf pattern rather than the figure eight; others included a "flag race, cutting contest, or even a roping competition."[170]

Lucyle bulldogging at the Houston Fat Stock Show. *Ralph R. Doubleday, circa 1935, nitrate negative. Ralph R. Doubleday Rodeo Photographs, Dickinson Research Center, National Cowboy & Western Heritage Museum. 79.026.0332.*

This contest, based two-thirds on horse quality and fancy costumes, led to another deviation from rodeo roots. Rodeo began as a working-class sport and remained so even after it became professional, but events judged on subjective qualities are vulnerable to bribery rather than athletic skill, resulting in separation from working-class contestants. This is proven in the sponsor girl contest, as "cowgirl athletes from the working class who excelled at [cutting, roping, and racing]…usually finished far behind the rich and the beautiful."[171] This relegated women out of professional competition as it had done since the end of the nineteenth century, limiting them to smaller amateur rodeos where they could still compete against cowboys in events like calf roping.[172]

While sponsor girls did promote rodeos, it was not in the traditional way that competing cowgirls had done previously. Rather than converting to pinup girls, cowgirls tried to keep their place in competition by sending a representative, Peggy Long, from the Cow Girl Bronk Riders to meet with the CTA. The result of the meeting was that the Cow Girl Bronk Riders joined on March 16, 1938, under the following conditions:

*The purposes for which we joined the Association are:*
*1ˢᵗ: To ride for a set price at all contract rodeos.*
*2ⁿᵈ: To reach an agreement with managers of contests as to rules and purses.*
*At all rodeos where Cow Girl Bronk Riding is [contracted] we have agreed to:*
*Rule #1. Ride a Bronk for not less than $15.00 at the small shows and for not less than $25.00 a mount at the larger shows.*
*Rule #2. To fine any Cow Girl Bronk Rider riding for less than the amount stated above. Fine set is $200.00 payable to Secretary, Turtle Association. $50.00 down and one fourth of all contract or contest money received until fine is paid. Any Cow Girl fined will be required to make down payment of $50.00 before any Turtle Cow Girl Bronk Rider will ride, either contract or contest at any rodeo with said Cow Girl.*[173]

As Turtles tried to negotiate fair wages and standardize prizes for select events, the cowgirls did the same. As CTA members, the cowgirl bronc riders asked Cleveland Rodeo Committee representative Maxwell McNutt for mount money. When McNutt contacted the CTA, he learned that the Turtles viewed the cowgirls as "honorary members" having no vote. Furthermore, CTA spokesman Everett Bowman stated that the girls would "have to stand on their own feet and sit in their own saddles," and McNutt rejected the cowgirls' request.[174] While the CTA turned its back on the cowgirls, outside the CTA, some cowboys continued to support cowgirls' competition.

In 1939 at the Fort Worth Stock Show rodeo, the producers canceled the cowgirl bronc riding competition and replaced it with the sponsor girls contest (called "ranch girls" at that rodeo). The cowboys there walked out, demanding officials add the cowgirls' bronc riding back into the program. The strike leader was Huey Long, whose wife, "Peggy Long was cowgirl bronc riding representative to the CTA."[175] The result was a feeble compromise to include a "two-woman bronc riding exhibition at one performance," which did not secure future bronc riding for women at the Fort Worth rodeo or help with expenses for the cowgirl bronc riders who had traveled to the rodeo expecting to ride for prize money.[176] Although things were changing for women athletes, they stayed involved in rodeo through clubs and amateur events and as promotional representatives.

Roundup clubs often provide training and experience for amateurs to transition into the next generation of professional rodeo stars, but during the 1930s and 1940s, the clubs also played an important part in sustaining rodeo. The Ada Round-Up Club began in 1938, and by 1941, it had three hundred members, a roping pen and a barn with stable facilities and "maintained a group of calves" for members to practice roping.[177] Representing the club, members participated in rodeo parades across Oklahoma and north Texas and each July would sponsor a contest to elect the Ada Rodeo Hostess Queen. To elicit interest from the region, any girl age sixteen to twenty-five could enter the contest. Most winners were from out of town. Contestants helped to raise money for the rodeo, earning votes for each dollar raised, and were also judged based on "30% for beauty and personality, 20% for riding and costume, 25% for horse and equipment, and 25% for riding ability."[178] The winner earned prizes often including a saddle donated by local businesses. Then she was to promote the club and the rodeo over the next year.

One well-recognized cowgirl from a similar club was Nancy Bragg Witmer. Nancy grew up near Tulsa and began trick roping in 1939. Her first big rodeo was in Chicago with a group of ten kids, all members of the Tulsa Mounted Troops. She was known for doing a backbend on the horse and then coming up into a Roman stand; it is now known as the Falling Tower trick.[179] As cover girl for *Spotlight* in 1948, she was reported to be "probably one of the youngest Tulsans to bring national fame to the oil Capitol."[180] In 1944, she earned a certificate while entertaining soldiers, receiving a commendation from the general in command of the New York Port along with Mickey Rooney. The publicity from the award landed her a four-year contract with Bob Wills and his troupe.[181] She was named the Roundup Girl of the month by Oklahoma Roundup in June 1946. These types of contests that extended beyond the local rodeo community created greater interest among families of girls involved in the queen contest. They also helped ensure crowds.

Efforts to keep crowds attending during the difficult war years found promoters placing heavy emphasis on patriotism and in support of the many cowboys who joined the military service. Overall, organizations like the Rodeo Association of America (RAA) encouraged rodeo committees to stress patriotic themes and broaden membership requirements so more amateurs could move up to professional status as a way to help sustain rodeo. Rodeo, as was the custom in the past, held benefit events to support the military or war effort and included war bonds as prizes. Women helped keep rodeo alive by filling in and entering competition in events they had recently been excluded from, except for in the all-girl rodeos. The first all-girl rodeo was organized by Fay Kirkwood at the Fannin County Fair Grounds in Bonham, Texas, from June 26 to 29, 1942.[182]

Nancy Bragg doing a backbend. *Ralph R. Doublday, circa 1935, nitrate negative. Ralph R. Doublday Rodeo Photographs, Dickinson Research Center, National Cowboy & Western Heritage Museum. 79.026.2767.*

Also producing all-girl rodeos was Vaughn Krieg. Vaughn was a rancher, competitor and rodeo producer who owned a ranch, raising cattle and horses.[183] She competed in professional rodeo in the late 1920s and early 1930s in four events: "calf roping, bronc riding, bulldogging, and steer riding."[184] Winner of the 1934 Madison Square Garden bronc riding championship, Vaughn herself was a contestant in Kirkwood's events.[185] Vaughn and her husband, Lynn Huskey, both had rodeo careers and owned a ranch near Towson, Oklahoma. The ranch, named the Flying V, had a rodeo arena, and they had produced Flying V Rodeos there annually since 1937. As they had both had successful careers in rodeo, the Flying V drew the most experienced cowboys and cowgirls on the circuit, who made the Flying V a success. Like other all-girl rodeos created in 1942 to entertain troops, Vaughn's Flying V All Cow-Girl Rodeo Company was planned to entertain at military bases. The program included "three contract acts, one sponsor contest, and six events....An all-star cast of rodeo hands competed in calf roping, wild cow milking, bronc riding, bulldogging, cutting, and steer riding. Among the participants were Marjorie Roberts, Ruth Roach,

Lucas, and Krieg herself who competed in bulldogging, bronc riding, calf roping, and steer riding."[186] Vaughn rodeoed a great deal in Oklahoma in Ada, Hinton, Muskogee, Tulsa, Mangum, Oklahoma City and Guthrie, to name a few, and was able to make a rodeo successful due to her reputation and ability to produce a quality rodeo. She was also interested in supporting the younger generation's interest in rodeo and developed a position in her rodeo for a mascot. Five-year-old Kaytricia Ann Pope from Bonham, Texas, rode a small pony named Tony and was a crowd favorite. Opening at the Lamar County Fair Grounds, near Paris, Texas, Vaughn organized the rodeo around patriotic themes, with the finale at the rodeo the "'V' for Victory" riding formation.[187]

Where rodeo displayed patriotic support, organizations like the Turtles did what they could financially to support the war effort by buying bonds, as much as "$10,000 worth," and waving fees for servicemen who could "disregard payment of dues if they were in any branch of the armed forces as they were exempt from paying dues for the duration of the war."[188] Communication with the rodeo family during the war was accomplished by women like the secretary for *Hooves & Horns* magazine, "Ma" Hopkins, who kept the cowboys serving abroad informed of rodeo news and of rodeo's support of the war effort. Similarly, she kept the fans informed about the cowboys as news came back from overseas and soldiers wrote to her with information.[189]

Vaughn Kreig on Slots. *Brown, 1924, gelatin silver print. Rodeo Photographs, Dickinson Research Center, National Cowboy & Western Heritage Museum. 88.9.1347.*

Vaughn Krieg and her husband, Lynn Huskey. *Ralph R. Doubleday, circa 1935, nitrate negative. Ralph R. Doubleday Rodeo Photographs, Dickinson Research Center, National Cowboy & Western Heritage Museum. 79.026.26993.*

Rodeo advertising placed patriotic duty at the forefront of community responsibility, as bold titles like "Rodeo Important to National Defense" indicate. The call for the rodeo community, contestants and fans alike, demanded reciprocal sacrifice. Programs encouraged the audience to support troops by reminding folks that part of the American heritage the men fought for included rodeo:

> *Rodeo will get short shrift under an axis regime. So, Rodeo is one thing we are fighting for, and it must be kept alive, as an integral part of our American way of living, for the duration. Wherever it's practicable the shows would go on. And after the active fighting is ended, it will again come into its own, for there is no other sport that so appeals to red blooded Americans.*
> *WE WILL WIN THE WAR.*
> *WE WILL HAVE RODEO.*[190]

Ruth Roach. *101 Ranch Collection, GM 4327.8542. Gilcrease Museum Archives.*

Advertising also incited fans to buy bonds with covers reading "Keep 'Em Flying! Keep 'Em Rolling! Buy War Bonds and Stamps! And On to VICTORY!!"[191]

Like many organizations across the United States that altered their purpose to include support of troops during World War II, these efforts proved challenging, perhaps doubly so in more sparsely populated regions like rural America. Entities like the Ada Fire Department were charged with added duties for civil defense purposes. For this reason, the Ada Fire Department (which had previously sponsored and produced the rodeo) decided not to have one in 1942. Instead, the Ada Round-Up Club and the Junior Chamber of Commerce hosted the event. Despite rations for gas and tires, many famous contestants took part in the rodeo. The band was provided by the Oklahoma State Prison in McAlester, and the Seminole Round-Up Club traveled to the rodeo on horseback. The clubs producing the rodeo were successful in keeping the rodeo going and awarded $8,500 in prizes, with half of that being war bonds. The year 1943 proved an even greater challenge, and the clubs opted to have a one-day rodeo limited to amateur athletes who competed for jackpot prizes. Again, the purpose was to try to sustain the rodeo through the war without detracting from patriotic duty. Professionals in the area put on exhibition matches, and famous rodeo clown John Lindsay worked the rodeo for expenses only. Although attendance was low, with a crowd of seven thousand for the one performance, again the clubs were successful in saving the rodeo.[192]

Women had taken the reins, so to speak, during the most difficult times of rodeo to help preserve it and to support America during its time of need for the duration of the war. Nevertheless, women competing professionally in rodeo almost ended completely. The last ladies' bronc riding event was in 1941 at Madison Square Garden in New York City. Oklahoma cowgirl Vivian White won. Vivian was born in Enid, Oklahoma, and first experienced horses used to farm in Ringwood. When she was fifteen, Vivian started her rodeo career riding exhibition steers and buffalo. She became a champion trick rider, traveling and

1941 Saddle Champ Vivian White. *Photographer undetermined, date not provided. National Cowgirl Museum and Hall of Fame, Fort Worth, Texas.*

rodeoing with her sister Grace, who made most of their costumes. Vivian was an exceptional bronc rider, having the "distinction of never being bucked off in the arena" over her eighteen-year rodeo career.[193]

Although women had helped create rodeo and had been superstars in the golden years, endured through the Depression and kept it going with all-girl rodeos during World War II, rodeo life for women after the war would not be the same. Once again, they would find the grit and determination to make their own way with their own professional organization.

## Chapter 5

# THE WOMEN'S PROFESSIONAL RODEO ASSOCIATION IN OKLAHOMA

The 1940s changed women's roles in mainstream rodeo in ways that reduced their presence and completely excluded them from competitive events, which had historically been so important in promoting and growing rodeo. To some extent, rodeo's heyday in the 1920s was due to the novelty of women roughstock riders and ropers as much as the fact that women excelled in rodeo competition. Regardless, women did not just go quietly into the night or even toward the spotlights that illuminated women's place in arena beauty pageants. As part of the change to rodeo that focused on women in non-athletic roles, rodeos like Gene Autry's shifted focus to beauty over ability and skill that cowgirls had long been known for. In 1942, one of the biggest rodeos, the Madison Square Garden Rodeo, "replaced the cowgirl bronc riders with 'sponsors' or 'glamor girls'—girls chosen from the western states to ride in the grand entry and barrel race...chosen more for glamor than talent...some of them could hardly ride." Some required riding lessons from the rodeo cowgirls.[194] Because professional cowgirls were now limited to one competition, the timed event of barrel racing, this new event category affected them and their career as well as the sponsor girls. The skills portion of the sponsor contests, however, had no written rules, resulting in inconsistency in judging as well as with placement of barrels. Girls reported that rodeo workers placed barrels "anywhere they wanted to any time they wanted to during the progress of the competition," and that also varied from rodeo to rodeo. Nancy Binford and Thena Mae Farr, who had participated in sponsor girl contests, began an all-girl rodeo as an alternative. True to ancestral cowgirls' grit, women formed their own professional organization: the Girls Rodeo Association, later the Women's Professional Rodeo Association (WPRA), which featured bareback bronc riding, breakaway calf roping, team roping, tie-down calf roping, barrel racing and bull riding, with the difference between men's and women's rules being that roughstock riding cowgirls were required to stay on for six seconds rather than the eight seconds for the men's roughstock events.[195] The mix of all-girl rodeos during this time included some shows that were exhibition performances and others strictly competitive rodeo like the GRA rodeos.

The evolution of all-girl rodeos that began during World War II, like the ones put on by Fay Kirkwood, were "primarily exhibition rather than competition."[196] This was the first of many rodeos produced by Kirkwood, with the last one held to entertain servicemen in Wichita Falls, Texas. After the war, women changed rodeo again. Unlike the all-girl exhibitions and Flying V contest, the new all-girls' rodeo would place cowgirls in competition in long-established rodeo events. The Flying V All-Cowgirl Rodeo put on by Vaughn Kreig offered competition for cowgirls contesting in "all of the traditional male events, including bull dogging and bull riding."[197] All-girl competitions and GRA rodeos were successful due in part to Kreig, Binford and Farr's extensive experience and connections in the rodeo community. In the case of Binford and Farr, who raised enough funds to cover the Beutler Bros. stock contractor fee of $1,000 and have "$1,260 in prize and mount money," the girls were able to draw contestants from several southwestern states to compete for a grand prize for the all-around champion: a horse trailer.[198] Also supporting this event were members of the rodeo family like the Regers.

The Regers from Woodward had a family history heavily involved in rodeo dating back to some of the first rodeos in the Panhandle. Regers had produced, announced and performed, with the whole family pitching in to make each rodeo a success. At the all-girls' rodeo in Amarillo, the Reger family worked to fill various jobs at the rodeo, from announcer to ticket office outside the arena. The girls, Dixie and Virginia, entertained in the arena with trick roping and trick riding, making it a family affair. The girls had been trick riders since before they were school-aged. Of the family, Dixie became well known as a rodeo clown and was later inducted into the hall of fame.

The rodeos produced by Binford and Farr became very popular, attracting "more publicity than those produced by males because they were really 'all-

Virginia and Dixie Reger trick riding. *T. Kaitila, date unknown, gelatin silver print. Monte Reger Rodeo Papers (care of Virginia Reger), Dickinson Research Center, National Cowboy & Western Heritage Museum. 1997.02744.*

girl,' down to the judges, clowns, and support staff."[199] Their first rodeo was in Amarillo on September 23–26, 1947.[200] When first approached about locating the rodeo in the Amarillo area, the Tri-State Fair Committee agreed to the event because after several years of decline in the traditional rodeo there, they believed this all-girl rodeo "would fill the grandstand and provide much-needed entertainment."[201] Much like the cowgirls from the 1900s to the 1930s, cowgirls in true competition indeed filled seats. The girls' rodeo drew veteran contestants who had proven careers in early rodeo like Vivian White, a rancher who raised white-faced cattle, Brahmas, registered Angus and quarter horses from Warner, Oklahoma, and rodeoed from 1927 to 1949. Vivian was fifteen years old when she began to rodeo in Cleo Springs, west of Enid. Her first rides were an exhibition ride on steer and one exhibition ride on buffalo. She continued doing exhibition steer riding in small towns across western Oklahoma for eight years before her first exhibition saddle bronc in St. Louis, Missouri, in 1935. Shortly thereafter, in 1936, she entered her first competition saddle bronc event in Indianapolis. She went on to win the 1937 Cowgirl Bronc Champ in Fort Worth, Texas, and the following year won the Trick Riding Championship in Cheyenne. That same year, she won the World Championship Ladies Saddle Bronc event at Madison Square Garden in New York City and repeated that victory again in 1941. In 1939 and 1941, she became the Champion Lady Bronc Rider of the Boston Garden Rodeo. In 1949, Vivian was riding in the GRA, where she won the Champion Saddle Bronc Rider in Texas. Her sister Gladys had taught her to ride broncs, and Vivian was reportedly never bucked off during any horse-riding competition in an arena. She became so well known for her talents that she also trained young trick riders, including famous Hollywood stuntwomen Shirley and Sharon Lucas.[202] Active in all aspects of rodeo, including riding at a Tornado Relief Rodeo at Pryor, Vivian was an avid competitor, charitable person and active in the agricultural community. As a member of the Black Angus Cattle Association for thirty years, the AQHA for forty years and the Cowboy Turtle and PRCA since 1937 with lifetime memberships, her legacy includes being known as the "greatest girl rider Oklahoma has ever produced."[203] Vivian and others like her helped make the girls' rodeos a success and inspired girls to take their endeavors one step further in their communities as well.

In response to the decision to limit women's athletic competition to only one event, barrel racing, and in protest of the beauty pageantry of sponsor girls, the GRA formed on February 28, 1948. Many women who formed the GRA had been part of the Tri-State All-Girl Rodeo. Like cowgirls of the past, doing what had to be done, forming their own organization and staging rodeos seemed a reasonable solution that would allow them to continue professional competition. As a professional organization, they elected officers: "Margaret Owens Montgomery as president; Dude Barton, vice president; and Mrs. Sid Pearson, secretary."[204] For the board of directors, the cowgirls voted in "Dixie Reger, Jackie Worthington, and Blanche Altizer, and

Rodeo parade with possibly Floyd Gale, Vivian White and Alice Adams leading a line of cowboys and cowgirls. *Ralph R. Doubleday, circa 1945, safety film negative. Ralph R. Doubleday Rodeo Photographs, Dickinson Research Center, National Cowboy & Western Heritage Museum. 79.026.3155.*

Madison Square Garden champion Vivian White," reflecting the Oklahoma and Texas area through board representation.[205]

The GRA established a point-scoring system like the RCA. One point was earned for each dollar won at GRA-sanctioned contests, and these points were totaled at the end of the season. The all-around champion cowgirl was the woman earning the highest points in two or more events. The GRA named the champions at the final all-girl rodeo at the season's end. With no age restrictions, any girl or woman could become a member. So as not to deprive younger members of the opportunity for growth or potential scholarships, girls in high school could be GRA members and still compete in high school rodeo. As adults, however, GRA members were prohibited from entering amateur or nonsanctioned rodeos. "The rules for all-girl rodeos included structure of entry fees and prizes, approval of promoters and producers, and rules of competition. The twelve events originally sanctioned included three each in roping and rough stock riding, four races, wild cow milking, and cutting."[206] The GRA began to offer a way to continue roughstock and other events that women had been professionally competing in for so many years before but also "to eliminate competitions based on beauty, costume, and arbitrary rules and replace them with standard, timed events."[207] Similar to the RCA, which enforced a strict dress code that required "cowboys to wear jeans, boots, hats, and long-sleeved cowboy shirts both in the arena and in publicity and program photos," appearance was standardized, as it was in other professional sports.[208] GRA-sanctioned rodeos required contestants to ride in the opening parades dressed in appropriate western-style button-down shirts, boots, hats and pants.

Veteran stars and a growing interest in girls' competition contributed to even greater popularity in smaller single events. For instance, a jackpot calf roping at Claude, Texas, in 1948 attracted a top field, including Fern Sawyer, Nancy Binford, Dude Barton, Jackie Worthington and Margaret Owens Montgomery. That started a trend through the mid-1950s of events like "matched calf roping, jackpot calf roping, and team roping" expanding in existing states where the GRA participated, as well as to new areas.[209]

In 1950, the GRA moved its headquarters to the Livestock Exchange Building in Fort Worth, Texas, to be nearer to the RCA headquarters. Working with the RCA to in one sense reintroduce professional cowgirls into rodeo, the GRA and the RCA in 1955 made an agreement and guidelines for that to happen:

> GRA president *Jackie Worthington* and RCA president *Bill Linderman* signed the following historic agreement still in effect today:
>
> Only Rodeo Cowboys' Association, Inc. cards will be honored by the Girls' Rodeo Association and the Rodeo Cowboys' Association, Inc., will strongly urge and recommend the use of G.R.A. girls in barrel racing in related events. In the case of straight rodeos, the Rodeo Cowboys' Association, Inc., will insist that such events conform to Rodeo Cowboys' Association, Inc. and G.R.A. rules and regulations.
>
> This agreement shall be in effect until such time as it is terminated by action of ether of the parties hereto.

The 1950s found women's rodeo had grown in size, with more than one hundred members and broader geographic coverage, as those members represented "eleven states and one Canadian province. By 1958, the GRA sanctioned barrel races in twenty-one states and Havana, Cuba, with purses totaling $27,924."[210] The new GRA publication, *Powder Puff and Spurs*, kept members and fans informed and had "622 subscribers in thirty-one states and Canada."[211] Women's rodeo was also published in the long-running

*Hoofs and Horns* and in Fog Horn Clancy's *Rodeo Histories and Records*, covering sanctioned events, GRA event winners and all-around champions.[212] The RCA publications *The Buckboard* and *Rodeo Sports News* also provided GRA standings and information.

Girls' rodeo also helped to inspire future generations. As stated previously, women have always contributed a great deal to rodeo as participants and in promoting the sport as a family event. Some, like Mary Lou Cravens, leave a legacy of champions who come up through the ranks of junior rodeo or Little Britches. Born in Coalgate, Oklahoma, Mary Lou was raised on a farm that also had sheep and cattle. On the family property, she and her brothers held amateur jackpot rodeos in an arena her brothers built. Rodeoing after business school, Mary Lou became an accomplished barrel racer, and by the 1960s, she was riding bulls too, retiring "undefeated."[213] Mary Lou was also an excellent trainer and became a champion barrel racer on a horse that was blind in one eye. She trained him to start the run to the left and found success winning an International Rodeo Association championship in 1964 and again in 1965. She again made it to the IRA finals in 1971. After retiring from competition in 1975, she served on the IPRA board of directors as the barrel racing director.[214] Both of her daughters, Johna and Dyana, barrel raced. Johna began in the Oklahoma Barrel Racing Association Junior Division but by the age of eight had earned her own IRA card.[215] Dayna was fifteen when she earned her IPRA card. Starting in youth rodeo, their parents traveled for the girls to compete. Many kids begin in junior rodeos or, like Dayna, in the Oklahoma High School Rodeo Association. "In 1979, she [Dayna] won the Oklahoma High School Barrel Racing Championship" and then advanced to the National High School Finals to barrel race before moving on to college rodeo.[216]

By that time, women's sports in general had become more well known to the public through TV and educational outreach, particularly after Title IX in 1972. Professional cowgirls knew the benefit this exposure could have for rodeo, and women like Sue Pirtle actively promoted GRA through this modern media. Sue was from Weatherford, and her accomplishments include competing in four events—calf roping, ribbon roping, bareback riding and bull riding—and winning eleven world titles as all-around cowgirl. Sue furthered cowgirls' image in the CBS *Challenge of the Sexes* in 1976–77, competing against the legendary Larry Mahan. In that match, Mahan was forced to ride his second bull to beat her and Chris LeDoux, and in 1977, she again made prime television coverage in ABC's *Women Superstars* program, finishing sixth overall. She became a technical advisor for the movie *Rodeo Girl* starring Katharine Ross in 1980, and she has been called "the most versatile cowgirl in the history of the GRA."[217] Her greatest contribution to rodeo might have been her efforts to promote the image of the modern cowgirl. She worked to increase exposure through "television, documentaries, sports competitions and movie appearances."[218] During her tenure on the WPRA board of directors and as director of the GRA, she increased awareness and interest in women's professional rodeo.[219]

Once retiring from professional rodeo careers, seldom do women cease to support the business. Women over the age of forty can also qualify for finals with the Senior Pro Rodeo and the National Senior Pro Rodeo Finals, sponsored by the National Old Timers Rodeo Association. Many others get into various aspects of rodeo business like raising livestock and horses. Another Oklahoma cowgirl who contributed to the legacy of women in rodeo was Euline Smith. Born and raised in Leedey, Oklahoma, Euline began her rodeo career in Leedey and the surrounding area. Although she rodeoed part time after marrying her husband, J.B., in 1955, by 1959, she had worked her way up to national ranking, being fifteenth in the Girls Rodeo Association. Her legacy did not end there, for after she retired in 1962, she continued to train barrel horses. Like other cowgirls, her whole family was involved in rodeo; her daughter both rides and trains barrel horses, and her grandsons are team ropers.[220]

The GRA and rodeo associates teaching kids and providing practice environments that mimicked professional rodeo in event categories, although with altered rules for safety and to instruct kids, resulted in some athletes excelling at a young age. Many GRA members also volunteer their time with organizations like the Red River Quarter Horse Association (RRQHA). The RRQHA was founded in 1959 by Rebecca Taylor Lockhart from Ryan, Oklahoma. Founded as a horse show just for the youth, it was the first of its kind, sponsoring youth quarter horse shows to help kids learn to show, rope and rodeo.[221] Not unlike Ann Lewis, who became a winner early on, another young cowgirl who broke records in 1977 was Jackie Jo Perrin. From Antlers, Oklahoma, Perrin rodeoed around her school schedule. She became the youngest rookie to win the GRA World Championship and rookie title, and the year she won, she became a star whom fans across the country loved. She went on to win a rodeo scholarship to Southeastern Oklahoma University in Durant and remains a favorite rodeo personality still recognized today.[222]

Many GRA professional cowgirls had to balance responsibilities at home, as they were often responsible for childcare when their children were of

Jackie Jo Perrin, the youngest rookie to win the GRA World Championship. *Photographer unknown, date unknown, gelatin silver print. Rodeo Photographs, Dickinson Research Center, National Cowboy & Western Heritage Museum. 88.9.1373.*

school age and no longer able to travel with their mothers. Like many men in early professional rodeo employed in full-time jobs to support their rodeo careers, women in the WPRA also worked outside of rodeo. Anita Smith was an accountant in Tulsa. She became interested in bull riding in "March of 1989 when she heard about a bull-riding school in Owasso." Although her father was a bull rider, she was twenty-six before she decided to try it herself. She was successful as a rookie and became one of the top female bull riders in the world.[223] Hoping to increase earnings for professional cowgirls, the GRA attempted to work with the RCA to level earnings for professional rodeo athletes.

In 1959, Billie McBride, GRA president, petitioned the RCA board to include barrel racing in the NFR. The NFR denied the request, and GRA finals took place at the RCA National Steer Roping Championship location in Clayton, New Mexico. The National Finals Rodeo Committee (NFRC) "recognized a need for some relief between six rounds of steer roping, and itself suggest that a barrel race would be the perfect solution." Also, still somewhat reminiscent of sponsor girls, the committee offered that the "women could provide the grand entry, pivots, hostesses, and color."[224] The following two years, 1960 and 1961, the GRA barrel racing finals moved to Scottsdale, Arizona, and Santa Maria, California, where the RCA team roping finals were also held.[225] In 1962, the barrel racing finals took place at Dallas, Texas, and the GRA held its finals separately. "During those years the RCA did make several concessions regarding holders of GRA and RCA cards, enabling women to compete in events sponsored by both organization and allowing women holding either GRA or RCA cards to compete in RCA-sanctioned team roping contests," but it would be six more years before barrel racing was added into the National Finals Rodeo.[226]

Much of the credit for incorporating barrel racers into the National Finals Rodeo is due to Florence Youree of Addington, Oklahoma. Youree had been negotiating this for some time before she achieved success in 1967, and even then, she had to provide the barrels.[227] Knowing that the well-liked barrel racing event would increase ticket sales, in 1967 the RCA board finally agreed to the GRA's request to include barrel racing in the National Finals. The stipulation from the RCA that the GRA be "willing to accept RCA cards as entries" seemed a minor technicality, when actually the NFR committee was so eager to hold the barrel race that it offered to put up the prize money itself to obtain approval. By a vote of eight to three, the board approved the inclusion of the event, with a $2,500 purse coming from the sponsors' half of the budget.[228] In reaction to the performance, officials proposed that the "GRA barrel racing finals be held at the NFR for as long as the rodeo was held in Oklahoma City [including] a minimum prize of $2,500," securing barrel racings future in the National Finals.[229]

The availability of barrel racing grew over the next decade, which helped promote rodeo to future generations. But within the professional organizations, balancing GRA and PRCA barrel racers could sometimes prove challenging. Betty Gayle Cooper, 1979 World Champion Calf Roper and well known and respected in all of rodeo, explained the challenges and issues that sometimes limited earnings for cowgirls, saying:

> *"Barrel racing is a part of the PRCA (Professional Rodeo Cowboys Assn.) rodeos. It's a flashy event. It cuts away monotony and it's popular with the spectators. I would like to see more money in all-girls rodeos. But, as far as being jealous that the barrel racers are included in the PRCA rodeos. I'm not!"* Cooper, the successful rodeo coach for Southeastern Oklahoma State University in Durant, would rather find a cure-all than indulge in sour grapes.[230]

Cooper knows how expensive travel is for all rodeo competitors, as she "has several male family members in her family in professional rodeo," but with women making a fraction of the earnings, she stated, "it's hard for the girls to get up enough added money for them to travel all over the country.... It's the same way with the PRCA. I would say the top five of each event travel extensively."[231] Promoting women's professional rodeo, Cooper is involved at all levels. As the American Junior Rodeo Association president from 1969 to 1971, she helped reorganize the association and developed rules and policies. Additionally, she coached the men's and women's rodeo teams for Southeastern Oklahoma State University (SOSU), working to educate and increase scholarship opportunities for younger athletes. At SOSU, in addition to coaching the rodeo teams, she teaches in the Equestrian Program and is the academic director of equine studies. During her time at SOSU,

Florence Youree making a turn. *Devere Helfrich, 1963, safety film negative. Devere Helfrich Rodeo Photographs, Dickinson Research Center, National Cowboy & Western Heritage Museum. 81.023.022187-11.*

she coached seven collegiate teams to the national finals. She also served as a women's judge for high school rodeo from 1984 to 1986 and for the youth association rodeos from 1979 to 1981. *Horseman Magazine* ran a series with Betty Gayle Cooper offering instruction for ladies' events. In December 1983, the topic was roping. Keeping with education in and about rodeo, she provided a detailed discussion about how to mentally prepare and then to practice for calf roping. Cooper's leadership and commitment to education improved women's professional rodeo.

As director, Cooper facilitated the move of the women's National Finals Rodeo to the Lazy *E* Arena in Guthrie in 1985. The move was a good choice in her mind: "'It's a great place for a rodeo,' says the Oklahoma native.... 'Everything is done first class.'"[232] The first finals drew only 2,700 people. But in 1987, the WPRA "established the Professional Women's Rodeo Association (PWRA), a separate division for all-women's events," increasing payouts to "$128,605 in prizes, $3,000 at the finals rodeo."[233] By 1989, "5,600 fans showed up during the three-night run in 1989, including a record 3,000 on the final night."[234] The year 1989 was also the first time the PWRA finals were televised. As A.G. Meyers, special events coordinator for the Lazy *E*, noted, "That is great for the rodeo and also for Oklahoma....A lot of people will see the show and it is great exposure for the state."[235] Reaching broad audiences, cowgirls not only inspired future generations but also developed training programs to help girls learn and succeed.

Women continue to promote rodeo and establish schools to train future athletes. Kay Vamvoras Young from Overbrook got her start through junior rodeo and the Little Britches Rodeo Association, where she rode bareback and bulls and did breakaway roping, barrels and poles before advancing in the high school division to the National High School Rodeo finals in barrels. Kay was twelve years old when she earned her GRA permit. She worked other jobs to earn entry fees and traveled to rodeos by working "racehorses, buying training and selling barrel horses."[236] Her father, Bill, trained horses and taught Kay as well as encouraged her to compete. She started barrel racing at age seven, attending a clinic by Florence Youree in Fort Collins, Colorado. Of the students who attend the Youree barrel racing and horsemanship camp, which she started in 1962, "90 per cent of the students have been girls. Few have had any background dealing with livestock, and most of the exceptions have been children of parents with huge ranch operations."[237] Youree introduced Kay to "form function in training, the belief that everything you do as a rider has an effect on what your horse does as an athlete."[238] This combined with Kay's natural talent led to her reputation as a cognizant and practical trainer whose hands-on approach at barrel clinics included her riding each horse personally to evaluate it. Her successful clinics have been held across the United States and in Brazil.[239]

She helped the GRA grow to more than "600 full-fledged members." During her time in the GRA, her goal was to work for women athletes to earn equal money with the men in their events. She promoted this idea through the existing interest in barrel racing.[240] Kay became a leader in barrel racing, serving on the board of directors for the Barrel Futurities of America for a total of nineteen years as well as being a director for the Turquois Circuit.[241] As president of the Women's Professional Rodeo Association in 1977, she selected for her vice president well-known rodeo personality and former rodeo queen Pam Minnick. They worked together, advocating for barrel racers to get equal pay in rodeo by creating a twenty-minute film campaign for such change, showing that the popularity of barrel racing was second only to bull riding. More "equal money barrel races" were added because of their film.[242]

Young advanced to the National Finals Rodeo in 1967 and in 1968 won second, having trained the horse she won on. This increased her reputation as a trainer, which led to great demand for her horses. Late in the rodeo season in 1969, she sold her horse and then "bought a horse used for steer wrestling and went right on winning. That year she ranked fourth at the NFR."[243] In 1985, she won the BFA World Championship. An exceptional trainer, Kay has been to the National Finals nine times on six different horses, partially because she is perpetually training.[244] She was inducted into the National Cowgirl Hall of Fame in 2009.

The Women's Professional Rodeo Association is the "oldest women's sports association in the United States and the only one governed entirely by women."[245] Now having their own finals each October and as part of the National Circuit Finals and the PRCA Wrangler National Finals Rodeo (WNFR), "WPRA barrel racers compete for millions of dollars each year." Still focused on the future, the WPRA in 2007 added a Junior World Champion Barrel Racer to its juniors' division for "ladies under the age of 18."[246] With over 2,500 members, the membership has grown "across the entire United States, as well as several Canadian provinces, and even Australia."[247] From support of military troops during wartime to supporting themselves in their own professional occupations as rodeo cowgirls, women in the GRA and the WPRA found a way to sustain their important roles in rodeo. Today, their great legacy is evident in the continuation of women in professions that lead new generations into rodeo competition, equine industry and research and into the new century of ranching to continue the way of life in rural Oklahoma.

# Chapter 6

# CONTEMPORARY COWGIRLS
# AND THE FUTURE

The popularity of rodeo has steadily grown, and the momentum rodeo gained from centralizing the Finals has really not slowed since the turning point of moving the National Finals Rodeo in Oklahoma City in the 1960s. Rodeo has divided, organized and specialized over the years to improve the quality of competition of the athletes, human and animal, and to help audiences better understand what they are experiencing through added education programs and inclusion of history into the rodeo program. The increased publication through television and added prize money through commercial sponsorships add to live rodeo an additional fan base of millions. Most recently, the sport has modernized with two new networks that carry rodeo online as well, RFDTV and the Cowboy Channel. The biggest changes for modern cowgirls transpired after the WPRA worked to improve payout amounts. From the 1960s' average earnings of $7,500, it jumped to $22,000 in the 1970s. Since 1980, the champion has earned at least $40,000 annually. The Professional Women's Rodeo Association, by awarding "$128,605 in prizes, $3,000 at the finals rodeo," helped to ensure the success of the finals and that they were televised. The event helped women in rodeo reach broader audiences.[248] The all-time high was $152,000, earned by Charmayne James in 1986, one of two seasons in which she earned more than the second- and third-place finishers combined. By the 1990s, world champion barrel racers earned an average of $111,170.[249] These gains, while an improvement, have not closed the gap, and women are still working to equalize the prize money for their singular event, which consistently remains the most popular with fans.

Coming back around full circle to the ranching that created the cowgirl, there are an increasing number of ranching women; women make up 33 percent of the agricultural industry today. Exceptional in improving and promoting ranching is Terry Stuart, who lives on and manages one of the oldest family ranches in Oklahoma. The Stuart Ranch started on land in Indian Territory in 1868.[250] The ranch is "38,000 acres of native rangeland, improved pasture and wheat pasture in three counties. The Blue River division, near Caddo, includes the original homestead and 16,000 acres. The Waurika division is a recent acquisition of 22,000 acres, 120 miles west of Caddo. Between the two, the Stuart Ranch runs 1,400 cows and about 1,800 stocker cattle."[251] Terry grew up on the ranch, began working it at age four and has managed it since 1976. This ranch is raising cattle and horses and is involved in ranch rodeo, leading the Oklahoma Range Roundup (the Oklahoma Cattlemen's Association annual ranch rodeo). An active member of the AQHA since 1981, Terry is very involved in breeding and showing quality quarter horses. The ranch uses its show horses to work, as all cattle on the ranch are worked on horseback. In 1995, Terry had one horse, Genuine Redbud, win the World Show Superhorse title and another, Genuine Hombre, make finalist in the calf roping.[252] The ranch's horses have won in various world shows and also in team roping with Zans Misty Gold, which earned "Superiors in heading, heeling and calf roping, and more than once been named 'Top Horse' at the Oklahoma Cattlemen's Association Range Roundup."[253] This earned Terry feature spots in publications by the Oklahoma Cattlemen's Association, *Western Horseman* and *The Cattleman*. Additionally, in 1996 the ranch received the "Best Remuda Award, given by AQHA and the National Cattleman's Beef Association to outstanding ranch remudas of registered American Quarter Horses."[254] This variety of awards does not come without a great deal of work on and off the ranch.

Terry has an animal science degree from Oklahoma State University and a graduate certificate from the Texas Christian University Ranch Management Program. She has earned awards for breeding and training horses as well as improved grazing and grassland, proving she is truly working for better ranching. In 2003, this was acknowledged with the awarding of the Range Management and Grassland Award. Terry also consults for the Sam Roberts Noble Foundation in Ardmore, a foundation dedicated to preserving and improving land. Terry's service is a testament to her dedication to ranching and preserving the land. A board member of the Oklahoma Cattlemen's Association from 1996 to 2000, she has also served on the Dean's Advisory Committee for Oklahoma State University (since 2002), on the National Beef Cattlemen's Association from 1992 to the present and on the National Cowboy & Western Heritage Museum board of directors from 2003 to the present, among many others. Her involvement and commitment to ranching and raising quarter horses preserve the very foundation and heritage of rodeo.

Rodeo has always been grounded in ranching, family, community and hard work. I had the privilege to watch Mary Burger win the Calgary Stampede in 2016. Mary is a self-employed barrel horse trainer who moved to Oklahoma in 1986 and lives in Paul's Valley. She started riding horses at a young age and won the 1974 inaugural World Champion Junior Barrel Race and pole bending at the AQHA on a horse, High Bars Wimpy, that she trained for the junior horse division competition.[255] Mary has since gone on to win ten world championships and nine AQHA world championships and was a PRCA/WPRA National Finals Rodeo qualifier in 2006, 2008 and 2009.

Mary Burger making a turn at Calgary Stampede, where she won the championship in July 2016. *Photo by author.*

Mary Burger's horse waits calmly in the alley at Calgary Stampede, July 2016. *Photo by author.*

Mary also portrays the greatest continuing quality in rodeo: determination. If you work hard enough to be good at what you do and have the heart for it, you can accomplish a great deal in the arena and, like cowgirls described in this book, can become an exceptional talent. Mary is the oldest athlete to qualify for the NFR and in 2016 earned the highest winnings of all cowboys and cowgirls, securing the privilege to wear back #1. She won a second world championship at the National Finals Rodeo at the age of sixty-eight and became one of only three barrel racers to wear the #1 back number.

Today, rodeo and equine industries continue to be a significant part of life in Oklahoma, contributing to the economy and preserving a diverse culture. Although the Indian National Finals, National Rodeo Finals and Ram National Circuit Finals rodeos have all moved out of Oklahoma, the state continues to offer important support to the rodeo industry through equine research, hosting a variety of weekly rodeos and rodeo schools and continuing to improve and expand agricultural support and education for the rodeo business. Furthermore, plans to build a new arena and show barn seem to indicate a sustained interest—perhaps one that will once again return various Finals events to Oklahoma, where the center of the western lifestyle is. But as women once again are edging back into various professional-level rodeo events, both roughstock and timed events—the addition of breakaway roping is a start—and earning their professional cards, it just may be the women who have always supported rodeo who make it come back full circle to once again be the sport that represents the equality and determination that built ranching in the American West.

# NOTES

## *Introduction*

1. A note about cowgirls—many around the world have appropriated the cowgirl spirit or persona. This often occurs when evoking extra courage to accomplish a particularly daunting task, someone who "gets their cowgirl on" or finds it necessary to "cowgirl up" to finish an undertaking. But historically and even today throughout much of the American West, the term *cowgirl* is reserved for one who either works with horses or ranches using horses or one who rodeos. Some women in this book might not have considered themselves cowgirls; for example, the rodeo secretary does not have to work cattle or ride horses on a regular basis and therefore might not call herself a cowgirl, but much of the outside world would because of her affiliation with rodeo life.

## *Chapter 1*

2. The National Finals Rodeo is the season-end finale of the Professional Rodeo Cowboy Association (PRCA) to compete for a world championship title. Points are based on winnings earned all season. The top fifteen high-point contestants compete at the NFR for ten days to determine the final world champion.
3. Porter, "American Rodeo," 42–43.

4. Ibid.

5. Everett, "Ranch Rodeo."

6. Rigging is the saddle, flank strap and gear used for saddle bronc riding. Roughstock refers to the bucking events: bareback bronc riding, saddle bronc riding and bull riding.

7. Everett, "Ranch Rodeo."

8. This statement is based on the suggestion (there is no true consensus among historians about the first rodeo) that the earliest rodeo was in Pecos, Texas, in 1883. The professionalization of rodeo here marks the creation of the Cowboy Turtle Association (CTA) in 1936. Early attempts to professionalize rodeo like the Wild Bunch in 1915 were foundational to the success of the CTA, but the CTA is the organization that eventually lasted.

9. Westermeier, *Man, Beast, Dust*, 289.

10. Athletes can compete at any PRCA-sanctioned rodeo to earn points for the NFR; however, because the NFR—which has larger prize payouts than most all other rodeos—is based on annual earnings, rodeo families now have to travel to be in larger rodeos outside their circuit and in addition to those in order to compete to be in the Finals.

11. Green, *Panhandle Pioneer*, 55.

12. Ibid.

13. Ibid.

14. Weaver, "Rodeo."

15. Fredriksson, *American Rodeo*, 175.

16. Trick and fancy roping "came from the *charro* riders of Old Mexico, such as Vincente Oropeza, who in 1894 introduced the *floreo de reata*, making flowers of rope." Groves, *Ropes, Reins, and Rawhide*, 4; Green, *Panhandle Pioneer*, 88.

17. Green, *Panhandle Pioneer*, 137.

18. Ibid., 172.

19. Ibid., 175.

20. Weaver, "Rodeo."

21. Ibid.

22. Fredriksson, *American Rodeo*, 106.

23. Ibid.

24. Ibid.

25. Ibid., 111.

26. Oklahoma is listed second behind Texas in the United States in total number of quarter horses. State size, state.1keydata.com/states-by-size.php.

27. Hiney, "Oklahoma Horse Industry Trends."

28. Ibid.
29. Ibid.
30. Ibid.
31. Ibid.
32. Ibid.
33. According to LeCompte, in 1993, "more than 85 percent of professional cowgirls still come from the old cattle frontier." LeCompte, *Cowgirls of the Rodeo*, 21.
34. Playdays are competitions organized for kids. Events often include barrel racing, goat tying, poles, ribbon racing or undecorating and roping.
35. The Cowboy Hall of Fame changed its name to the National Cowboy & Western Heritage Museum in 2000. Groves, *Ropes, Reins, and Rawhide*, 151.
36. Santos, *The Finals*, 8–16.
37. Ibid.
38. Ibid., 20.
39. Historically, re-rides took place after the regular competition rounds of the last event, bull riding, were complete. Then, any event in which a re-ride was granted (an offer made by the individual judges of each event competition) would take place, often in the same order as events during the rodeo. So, a saddle bronc re-ride would take place before a bull riding re-ride. The decision to offer a re-ride can be subjective and is at the discretion of the judges who sometimes will allow the option due to gate malfunction or if the animal just refuses to buck. The decision to accept a re-ride is the athlete's to make. Even if earning a low score, an athlete can re-ride to attempt to earn a higher score if that is an option. Today, if a re-ride is offered, it often occurs at the end of the regular competition for that specific event instead of at the end of the rodeo.
40. Myrtis Dightman quoted in Santos, *The Finals*, 36. Myrtis Dightman qualified for the NFR six times.
41. Ibid.
42. Ibid.
43. Of all the events that have been criticized by animal rights advocates, steer roping has remained the most scrutinized. Although many rule changes have been implemented to better protect the steers, it still remains controversial and separate from the highly publicized NFR in Las Vegas.
44. Clem McSpadden quoted in Santos, *The Finals*, 40. Clem McSpadden was voted the PRCA Announcer of the Year in 1986 and inducted into the ProRodeo Hall of Fame in 1990.

45. "Go-round" refers to the daily winner or top-scoring contestant. Although points earned for the entire ten rounds or days determine the NFR world champion, the top winner of the day also earns prize money for that day. Leo Camarillo quoted in Santos, *The Finals*, 60. Leo Camarillo has five world titles and six NFR average titles and has qualified for the NFR twenty times. The ProRodeo Hall of Fame inducted him in 1979.

46. Leo Camarillo quoted in Santos, *The Finals*, 60.

47. Santos, *The Finals*, 79.

48. Leo Camarillo quoted in Santos, *The Finals*, 60.

49. Don Gay quoted in Santos, *The Finals*, 82. Don Gay has eight bull riding world titles and one NFR average title and has qualified for the NFR thirteen times. He was inducted into the ProRodeo Hall of Fame in 1979.

50. Pro Rodeo Cowboy Association, "About the PRCA."

51. Everett, "National Finals Rodeo."

52. Pro Rodeo Hall of Fame, "RAM National Circuit Finals Rodeo."

53. Stratton, *Chasing the Rodeo*, 4–5.

54. Ibid., 1–2.

55. Ibid., 19.

56. Wolf, "In Depth: Rodeo History."

57. Ibid.

58. Ibid.

59. The city recently announced plans for a new 277,600-square-foot coliseum expected to be most used for equestrian events. One must wonder if they will try again for the next bid to relocate the NFR and bring it back to Oklahoma. Crum, "Coliseum Envisioned for State Fair Park."

60. Green, *Panhandle Pioneer*, 177.

## Chapter 2

61. Wallis, *Real Wild West*, 269.

62. Ibid., 270.

63. Lucille's parents were both orphaned. Zack was only eight when he was taken in by an aunt and uncle, Joseph Mulhall (Irish Catholic in St. Louis). Later, Mary Agnes, also a relative, was brought to live with them. Zack took the Mulhalls' name, studied for a few semesters at the University of Notre Dame, played for the St. Louis Empires and worked on the livestock ferries on the Mississippi before starting work for the railroad. Mary Agnes was twelve years younger than Zack and attended Saint Mary's

College at Notre Dame (a liberal arts school for women). They married in 1875 when Zack was twenty-eight and Mary Agnes was sixteen. Zack and Mary Agnes had four sons and four daughters; all but three died as infants (including twin girls who died in infancy), leaving son Logan (who was fourteen when he died of diphtheria), Agnes "Bossie" and Lucille. Zack and mistress Georgia (an orphan who worked at the boardinghouse where Zack stayed when working for the Santa Fe Railroad) had a son together, Charles Joseph, born in 1888. When Charley was ten years old, Zack moved him to live with the rest of the family in St. Louis. The second child born to Zack and Georgia in 1895 was a daughter, also given to Mary Agnes to raise. She named her Mildred Madeline after the dead twins. Wallis, *Real Wild West*, 223.

64. A cinch is a strap that holds a saddle on a horse, secured either by tying the cinch strap through a saddle ring or securing it with a buckle.

65. Stansbury, *Lucille Mulhall*, 7; Acton, "Lucille Mulhall," 6–7.

66. Wallis, *Real Wild West*, 224.

67. Olds, "Mulhall Ranch," 4.

68. Ibid., 5.

69. Ibid.

70. Ibid.

71. Stansbury, *Lucille Mulhall*, 11.

72. In 1897, N.H. Gentry of Sedalia offered a resolution at the fifth annual Missouri Swine Breeders Association meeting in Lexington, encouraging the general assembly to establish a fair. On January 15, 1899, Representative C.E. Clark of Mexico introduced a bill, on recommendation from Governor Lon V. Stephens, creating a Missouri State Fair. The first Missouri State Fair was held on September 9–13, 1901. www.mostatefair.com/fair-history. The World's Fair was held in 1904 to commemorate the Louisiana Purchase.

73. Stansbury, *Lucille Mulhall*, 13.

74. Greer, "Programme for July 3rd."

75. There was a mix-up at the parade that caused Zack to lose some "prestige" back home when Mulhall's band, the Frisco Line Territorial Band, was supposed to escort the Grand Army of the Republic for the president's trip back to the White House. They went to sign in only to find their spot had been given to another group called the Oklahoma Rough Rider Band. Unable to resolve the conflict before the events began, the Frisco Band was placed with Vice President Teddy Roosevelt's escort. Stansbury, *Lucille Mulhall*, 17.

76. Wallis, *Real Wild West*, 230; Roach, *Cowgirls*, 85.

77. Wallis, *Real Wild West*, 231; Roach, *Cowgirls*, 85–86.

78. This is where Milt Riske puts the incident where her clothes are ripped off, rather than El Paso. Riske, *Those Magnificent Cowgirls*, 36.

79. Roach, *Cowgirls*, 86.

80. *New York Times*, "Cowgirls Ride Up Avenue."

81. Olds, "Mulhall Ranch," 9.

82. Carlile, *Buckskin, Calico & Lace*, 129.

83. Wallis, *Real Wild West*, 222.

84. Ibid., 245–46.

85. *Shea's Theatre Program*.

86. Golobie, *Oklahoma State Register*.

87. Ibid.

88. Carlile, *Buckskin, Calico & Lace*, 95.

89. Stansbury and Stansbury, *History of Mulhall*, 207; Wallis, *Real Wild West*, 245.

90. LeCompte, *Cowgirls of the Rodeo*, 62.

91. Ibid.

92. Olds, "Mulhall Ranch," 6.

93. LeCompte, *Cowgirls of the Rodeo*, 52.

94. Ibid., 58.

95. Norman, *State Journal*.

96. Wilson, "Sioux City, State Fair," 5.

97. LeCompte, *Cowgirls of the Rodeo*, 64–65.

98. Reynolds with Schein, *A Hundred Years of Heroes*, 118.

99. Ibid., 111.

100. Ibid., 115.

101. Ibid., 118.

102. Stansbury and Stansbury, *History of Mulhall*, 255.

103. LeCompte, *Cowgirls of the Rodeo*, 110–11.

104. Ibid., 38.

## *Chapter 3*

105. Wilson, "Muskogee Roundup," 14.

106. LeCompte, *Cowgirls of the Rodeo*, 67.

107. Lewis, "Cowgirl Recalls Early Days," 33.

108. Clancy, "Memory Trail."

109. LeCompte, *Cowgirls of the Rodeo*, 75.

110. Gray, "She Came a Long Way," 50.

111. Ibid.

112. Smith, "OK Cowgirls Remember Early Days of Rodeo."

113. Ibid.

114. Bell, "History IPRA."

115. Laegreid, *Riding Pretty*, 198.

116. Ibid., 199.

117. Clancy, "Arena Highlights," 87–88.

118. Ann Lewis collection, National Cowgirl Hall of Fame and Museum, Fort Worth, Texas.

119. Santos, *The Finals*, 44–45; Mankin, "Tragic Day in Barrel Racing."

120. Groves, *American Horse*, 33.

121. Santos, *The Finals*, 220.

122. Klepper, *Ada Rodeo*, 2–3.

123. Ibid., 3–4.

124. Klepper, *Ada Rodeo*, 14.

125. Ibid., 16.

126. Goodspeed, *Cowboy Sweethearts*, 160.

127. Ibid., 121.

128. Ibid., 123.

129. Ibid., 124.

130. Ibid., 93.

131. Ibid., 107.

132. Ibid., 109.

133. Ibid., 39.

134. Ibid., 39–40.

135. Ibid., 147.

136. Goodspeed, *Cowboy Sweethearts*, 172–74.

137. Lamb, *R-O-D-E-O Back of the Chutes*, 11.

138. Ibid., 47.

139. Ibid., 48–49.

140. Ibid., 50.

141. Ibid., 50–51.

142. The Cowboy Alumni Association was "formed in 1988 to support and promote the sport of rodeo as well as to keep former contestants, fans, and friends in touch with each other." Goodspeed, *Cowboy Sweethearts*, 52.

143. Ibid., 15.

144. Ibid., 18.
145. Ibid., 19.
146. Ibid., 23.
147. Ibid., 24.
148. Ibid.
149. Austin and Austin, "2006 Hall of Fame Inductee Vicki Herrera Adams."

## *Chapter 4*

150. LeCompte, *Cowgirls of the Rodeo*, 101.
151. Ibid.
152. Ibid.
153. Roach, *Cowgirls*, 93.
154. Ibid.
155. Clancy, "Memory Trail."
156. Ibid.
157. Gray, "She Came a Long Way," 44. Note sometimes her name is listed in rodeo programs as Princess Mohawk and other times as Florence Hughes Randolph.
158. Ibid., 140.
159. Klepper, *Ada Rodeo*, 72.
160. Gray, "She Came a Long Way."
161. Oklahoma had started the Oklahoman Milk and Ice Fund in 1914 to help poor families have milk and ice for refrigeration. This program lasted in Oklahoma until 1953. Minty, "Milk and Ice Fund Early Charity." The charity the cowgirls contributed to in New York was part of a WPA program organized through the mayor of New York at that time.
162. Cohen, "Lucyle Roberts, 'Queen of Saddle.'"
163. Ibid.
164. Emorésa and De Anda, "Plaza de Toros."
165. LeCompte, *Cowgirls of the Rodeo*, 107.
166. Ibid.
167. Cohen, "Lucyle Roberts, 'Queen of Saddle.'"
168. LeCompte, *Cowgirls of the Rodeo*, 110.
169. Ibid., 118.
170. Ibid., 115.
171. Ibid.
172. Ibid., 116.

173. Woerner, *Cowboys' Turtle Association*, 99.

174. Ibid., 101–2.

175. LeCompte, *Cowgirls of the Rodeo*, 119.

176. Ibid.

177. Klepper, *Ada Rodeo*, 18.

178. Ibid., 19.

179. Nancy Bragg Witmer collection, 5.

180. Ibid., 7.

181. Ibid., 28.

182. LeCompte, *Cowgirls of the Rodeo*, 129.

183. *Bonham Daily Favorite*, "Vaughn Kreig to Participate in All-Girl Rodeo," 5.

184. Laegreid, *Riding Pretty*, 185.

185. LeCompte, *Cowgirls of the Rodeo*, 131.

186. Ibid., 131–32.

187. Krieg, *Flying V Rodeo*.

188. Woerner, *Cowboys' Turtle Association*, 164, 178.

189. Ibid., 165.

190. Ibid.

191. Krieg, *Flying V Rodeo*.

192. After the war, the rodeo grew. Festivities and events expanded to include an Oklahoma Quarter Horse Association show and sale. By 1947, the Ada Rodeo was billed as the second-largest outdoor rodeo in the world, and by 1958, it was ranked fifth in the United States. Klepper, *Ada Rodeo*, 10–11, 16.

193. Ibid., 89.

## *Chapter 5*

194. Jordan, *Cowgirls*, 238.

195. Morris, "Mama Was a Bull Rider," 10.

196. Klepper, *Ada Rodeo*, 29.

197. Ibid.

198. LeCompte, *Cowgirls of the Rodeo*, 149–50.

199. Ibid., 168.

200. Ibid., 148.

201. Ibid., 149.

202. Shirley Lucas Jauregi is from Bartlesville, Oklahoma, and became a trick rider and stuntwoman. She and her sister Sharon started exercising

horses for local oil executives and got into rodeo by running ribbons for cowboys at the Round-Up Club and nearby rodeos in Dewey and Vinita. Their mom contacted Don Wilcox in Tulsa to teach the girls trick riding, but he passed them off to Vivian White in Nowata. From trick riding in rodeos, they went on to become stunt doubles in movies such as *Montana Belle*, *Annie Get Your Gun* and *Westward the Women*.

203. *Bonham (TX) Daily Favorite*, June 23, 1942.
204. LeCompte, *Cowgirls of the Rodeo*, 154.
205. Ibid.
206. Ibid., 156.
207. Ibid.
208. Ibid., 157.
209. Ibid., 162–63.
210. Ibid., 159.
211. Ibid.
212. Ibid.
213. Klepper, *Ada Rodeo*, 44.
214. The IRA changed its name to the International Professional Rodeo Association, or IPRA, in 1983.
215. Klepper, *Ada Rodeo*, 45.
216. Ibid., 46.
217. Sue Pirtle collection.
218. Klepper, *Ada Rodeo*, 71.
219. Ibid.
220. Ibid., 80.
221. Tyler, "Family Affair," 80.
222. Nelson, "Where Are They Now?"
223. Morris, "Mama Was a Bull Rider," 10.
224. LeCompte, *Cowgirls of the Rodeo*, 176.
225. Ibid.
226. Ibid.
227. *Women's Pro Rodeo News*, "WPRA Celebrates 26th Birthday," 12.
228. LeCompte, *Cowgirls of the Rodeo*, 177.
229. Ibid., 178.
230. Young, "Cooper Speaks Up," 12.
231. Ibid.
232. Morris, "Mama Was a Bull Rider," 10.
233. LeCompte, *Cowgirls of the Rodeo*, 191.
234. Morris, "Mama Was a Bull Rider," 10.

235. Ibid. Note that at this time the women's profession organization was called PWRA for Women's Professional Rodeo Association; it was later changed to WPRA.
236. Kay Whittaker Young collection.
237. Sharrock, "Youngsters Learn Barrel Racing," 12b.
238. Hill. "Celebrating a Survivor," 46.
239. Dane, "Philosophies of Ms. President Kay Vamvoras," 5.
240. Ibid.
241. Hill, "Celebrating a Survivor," 48.
242. Ibid., 50.
243. Beel. "Barrel Racer 'Born and Raised on a Horse.'"
244. Hill, "Celebrating a Survivor," 50; Travis, "Kay Young," 7.
245. Gillum, "Inside the Women's Professional Rodeo Association."
246. Ibid.
247. Ibid.

## *Chapter 6*

248. LeCompte, *Cowgirls of the Rodeo*, 191.
249. Ibid., 180.
250. Groves, "Stuarts of the Land," 41.
251. Ibid., 42.
252. Ibid.
253. Ibid.
254. Ibid., 41.
255. Now for horses under age five.

# BIBLIOGRAPHY

Acton, Mildred Mulhall. "Lucille Mulhall—the Original Cowgirl." *The Ranchman* 1, no. 10 (February 1942): 6–7.

Austin, Jim, and Gloria Austin. "2006 Hall of Fame Inductee Vicki Herrera Adams." National Multicultural Western Heritage Museum. www.cowboysofcolor.org/profile.php?ID=18.

Bakken, Gordon Morris, ed. *Icons of the American West: From Cowgirls to Silicon Valley.* Vol. 1. Westport, CT: Greenwood Press, 2008, 89.

Beel, Marianne. "Barrel Racer 'Born and Raised on a Horse.'" Kay Young collection. National Cowgirl Museum and Hall of Fame, Fort Worth, Texas.

Bell, Don. "History IPRA." International Professional Rodeo Association. www.ipra-rodeo.com/history.

*Bonham (TX) Daily Favorite,* June 23, 1942. Vivian Gladys White Dillard collection, National Cowgirl Hall of Fame, and Museum, Fort Worth, Texas.

———. "Vaughn Kreig to Participate in All-Girl Rodeo." June 23, 1942, 5.

Carlile, Glenda. *Buckskin, Calico & Lace: Oklahoma Territorial Women.* Stillwater, OK: New Forums Press Inc., 2008.

Clancy, Fog Horn. "Arena Highlights." *Thrills in Rodeo,* n.d., 87–88.

———. "Memory Trail." *Hoofs and Horns,* January 8, 1942.

Cohen, Sam. "Lucyle Roberts, 'Queen of Saddle,' Rides Here." *New York Times,* November 1934.

Crum, William. "Coliseum Envisioned for State Fair Park as City Considers MAPS 4 Ideas." *The Oklahoman*, February 25, 2019. newsok.com/article/5623903/coliseum-envisioned-for-state-fair-park.

Dane, Claudia. "Philosophies of Ms. President Kay Vamvoras Leaves a Job Well Done." *Girls Rodeo Association*, January 1978, 5.

Emorésa, S. Estavillo, and J. De Anda. "Plaza de Toros." Lucyle Roberts collection. National Cowgirl Hall of Fame and Museum, Fort Worth, Texas.

Everett, Dianna. "National Finals Rodeo." Encyclopedia of Oklahoma History and Culture. www.okhistory.org/publications/enc.php?entry=NA008.

———. "Ranch Rodeo." Encyclopedia of Oklahoma History and Culture. www.okhistory.org/publications/enc.php?entry=RA011.

Fredriksson, Kristine. *American Rodeo from Buffalo Bill to Big Business*. College Station: Texas A&M University Press, 1993.

Gillum, Amy. "Inside the Women's Professional Rodeo Association." *Cowgirl Magazine*, December 17, 2014. cowgirlmagazine.com/wpra.

Golobie, John. *Oklahoma State Register*. December 31, 1914. Gateway to Oklahoma History. gateway.okhistory.org/ark:/6731/metadc169470.

Goodspeed, Judy. *Cowboy Sweethearts*. Edmond, OK: Dragonfly Publishing Inc., 2006.

Gray, Sally. "She Came a Long Way to Claim a Spot in the National Cowboy Hall of Fame." *The Quarter Horse Journal*, March 1971, 50, 54.

Green, Donald E. *Panhandle Pioneer: Henry C. Hitch, His Ranch, and His Family*. Norman: University of Oklahoma Press, 1979.

Greer, Frank H. "Programme for July 3rd." *Oklahoma State Capital*, July 3, 1900, 2. gateway.okhistory.org/ark:/67531/metadc124158.

Groves, Lesli. *American Horse*, September–October 1999, 33.

———. "Stuarts of the Land." *The Quarter Horse Journal*, December 1996, 42.

Groves, Melody. *Ropes, Reins, and Rawhide: All About Rodeo*. Albuquerque: University of New Mexico Press, 2006.

Hill, Breanne. "Celebrating a Survivor." *Barrel Horse News*, October 2009, 46.

Hiney, Kris. "Oklahoma Horse Industry Trends." *Oklahoma Cooperative Extension Service*. Stillwater: Oklahoma State University, 2018.

Jordan, Teresa. *Cowgirls: Women of the American West*. Lincoln: University of Nebraska Press, 1992.

Kay Whittaker Young collection. National Cowgirl Museum and Hall of Fame, Fort Worth, Texas.

Klepper, Ann. *The Ada Rodeo, an Incredible Saga*. Columbus, OH: PAST Foundation Inc., 2009.

Krieg, Vaughn. *Flying V Rodeo*. Official souvenir program, Paris, TX, 1942. Vaughn Krieg collection. National Cowgirl Hall of Fame and Museum, Fort Worth, Texas.

Laegreid, Renée M. *Riding Pretty: Rodeo Royalty in the American West*. Lincoln: University of Nebraska Press, 2006.

Lamb, Gene. *R-O-D-E-O Back of the Chutes*. Denver: Bell Press, 1956.

LeCompte, Mary Lou. *Cowgirls of the Rodeo, Pioneer Professional Athletes*. Urbana: University of Illinois Press, 1993.

Lewis, Kate. "Cowgirl Recalls Early Days." *Rodeo News*, May 1978, 20, 33.

Mankin, Julie. "Tragic Day in Barrel Racing." *Barrel Horse News*, August 23, 2018, reprinted from January 2007.

Minty, Chip. "Milk and Ice Fund Early Charity." *Oklahoman*, April 24, 1994. newsok.com/article/2464001/milk-and-ice-fund-early-charity.

Morris, Tim. "Mama Was a Bull Rider." *Oklahoma Today*, October 1990, 10.

Nancy Bragg Witmer collection. National Cowgirl Museum and Hall of Fame, Fort Worth, Texas, 5.

Nelson, Megan. "Where Are They Now?" *Barrel Horse News*, October 3, 2018. barrelhorsenews.com/barrel-racing-articles/throwback-thursday/where-are-they-now.

*New York Times*. "Cowgirls Ride Up Avenue: Col. Mulhall's Daughters, Who Ride Astride, Take the Air." April 24, 1905.

Norman, Floyd. *State Journal* (Mulhall, OK). October 23, 1914. Gateway to Oklahoma History. gateway.okhistory.org/ark:/67531/metadc141357.

Olds, Fred. "The Mulhall Ranch and Colonel Zack's Wild West Show Center in Story of Lucille." *The War Chief of the Indian Territory Posse of Oklahoma Westerners* 8, no. 3 (December 1974): 4.

Porter, Williard H. "The American Rodeo, Sport and Spectacle." *American West* 8, no. 4 (July 1971): 42–43.

Pro Rodeo Cowboy Association. "About the PRCA." www.prorodeo.com/prorodeo/rodeo/about-the-prca.

Pro Rodeo Hall of Fame. "RAM National Circuit Finals Rodeo." www.prorodeohalloffame.com/inductees/by-category/rodeo-committees/ram-national-circuit-finals.

Reynolds, Clay, with Marie-Madeleine Schein. *A Hundred Years of Heroes: A History of the Southwestern Exposition and Livestock Show*. Fort Worth: Texas Christian University Press, 1999.

Riske, Milt. *Those Magnificent Cowgirls: A History of the Rodeo Cowgirl*. Cheyenne, WY: Frontier Printing Inc., 1983.

Roach, Joyce Gibson. *The Cowgirls.* Denton: University of North Texas Press, 1990.

Santos, Kendra, ed. *The Finals: A Complete History of the First 50 Years of the Wrangler National Finals Rodeo, 1959–2008.* Colorado Springs, CO: Professional Rodeo Cowboys Association, 2009.

Sharrock, Tom. "Youngsters Learn Barrel Racing, Horsemanship." *Lawton Constitution-Morning Press,* July 5, 1964, 12b.

*Shea's Theatre Program.* Buffalo: Shea's Theatre, 1907.

Smith, Charlotte Anne. "OK Cowgirls Remember Early Days of Rodeo." 1985. Pauline Nesbitt collection, National Cowgirl Hall of Fame and Museum, Fort Worth, Texas.

Stansbury, Kathryn B. *Lucille Mulhall: Her Family, Her Life, Her Times.* N.p.: self-published, 1985.

Stansbury, Kathryn, and Max Stansbury. *History of Mulhall, Oklahoma 100 Yesteryears.* Norman, OK: Traditional Publishers, 1988.

Stratton, W.K. *Chasing the Rodeo, on Wild Rides and Big Dreams, Broken Hearts and Broken Bones, and One Man's Search for the West.* Orlando, FL: A Harvest Book Harcourt Inc., 2005.

Sue Pirtle collection. National Cowgirl Museum and Hall of Fame, Fort Worth, Texas.

Travis, Paul. "Kay Young." *The Barrel Racer,* December 1985, 7.

Tyler, Rebecca. "A Family Affair: The Red River Quarter Horse Association." *The Quarter Horse Journal,* May 1962, 80.

Wallis, Michael. *The Real Wild West: The 101 Ranch and the Creation of the American West.* London: Pimlico, 1999.

Weaver, Bobby D. "Rodeo." Encyclopedia of Oklahoma History and Culture. www.okhistory.org/publications/enc.php?entry=RO014.

Westermeier, Clifford P. *Man, Beast, Dust: The Story of Rodeo.* Denver: World Press Inc., 1947.

Wilson, Homer. "Muskogee Roundup." *Wild Bunch* 1, no. 4 (July 1915): 14.

———. "Sioux City, State Fair." *Wild Bunch* 1, no. 8 (November 1915): 5.

Woerner, Gail Hughbanks. *The Cowboys' Turtle Association: The Birth of Professional Rodeo.* Walnut Springs, TX: Wild Horse Press, 2011.

Wolf, Jeff. "In Depth: Rodeo History, Rodeo Roots." *Las Vegas Review-Journal,* December 9, 2001.

*Women's Pro Rodeo News.* "WPRA Celebrates 26th Birthday at the National Finals Rodeo." December 1993, 12.

Young, Carol. "Cooper Speaks Up." *World of Rodeo and Western Heritage,* October 1981, 12.

# INDEX

# ABOUT THE AUTHOR

 **D**r. Tracey Hanshew is an assistant professor at Washington State University, Tri-Cities. At WSU, she teaches U.S. history, upper division courses on women in the West and women in American society and an interdisciplinary course on Title IX. She is a Muriel H. Wright Award winner from the Oklahoma Historical Society for her article "Rodeo in Oklahoma Is Women's Business," published in the *Chronicles of Oklahoma*. She serves on the Advisory Board to *Americana: The Journal of American Popular Culture, 1900 to Present*, and is the membership and communication coordinator for the United States for the Rural Women's Studies Association. Dr. Hanshew is active in public history and community outreach, having been a guest speaker for the University of Calgary in Calgary, Alberta, and at regional museums across Oklahoma. Her presentations also include multiple international conferences in France and Canada and across the United States, where she has presented and served as a commentator and chair for history conferences as part of her dedication to and support of the field.